E G

FRANCE 1940

BLITZKRIEG

FRANCE 1940

ALAN SHEPPERD

First published in Great Britain in 1990 by Osprey Publishing, Elms Court, Chapel Way, Botley, Oxford OX2 9LP, United Kingdom.
Email: info@ospreypublishing.com

Also published as Campaign 3: *France 1940*

© 1990 Osprey Publishing Ltd.
00 01 02 03 04   10 9 8 7 6 5 4 3 2 1

Produced by DAG Publications Ltd for Osprey Publishing Ltd.

Revisions and tourist information by Martin Marix Evans

COVER: 10th Infantry Division in parade uniforms, Vienna, March 1938. (Brian Davis Collection)

Colour bird's eye view illustrations by Cilla Eurich.
Cartography by the Map Studio
Wargaming France 1940 by Colin Rumford.
Wargames consultant Duncan Macfarlane.
Typeset by Ronset Typesetters Ltd, Darwin, Lancashire.
Mono camerawork by M&E Reproductions, North Fambridge, Essex.

Key to Map Symbols

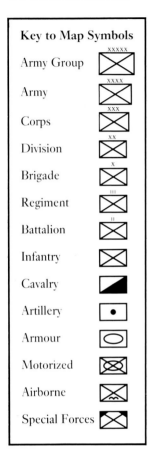

Army Group	XXXXX
Army	XXXX
Corps	XXX
Division	XX
Brigade	X
Regiment	III
Battalion	II
Infantry	
Cavalry	
Artillery	
Armour	
Motorized	
Airborne	
Special Forces	

FOR A CATALOGUE OF ALL BOOKS PUBLISHED BY OSPREY MILITARY, AUTOMOTIVE AND AVIATION PLEASE WRITE TO:

The Marketing Manager,
Osprey Direct USA, PO Box 130,
Sterling Heights, MI 48311-0130, USA.
Email: info@ospreydirectusa.com

The Marketing Manager,
Osprey Direct UK, PO Box 140,
Wellingborough, Northants,
NN8 4ZA, United Kingdom.
Email: info@ospreydirect.co.uk

Visit Osprey at:
www.ospreypublishing.com

Printed in China through
World Print Ltd.
Photographs in this volume are
reproduced by courtesy of the
Imperial War Museum, London.
Prints are available on application to
the Department of Photography,
Imperial War Museum, Lambeth
Road, London SE1. The Visitors'
Room is open to the public by
appointment.

ISBN 1 84176 037 4

CONTENTS

French troops building an
anti-tank ditch north of
the Maginot Line.

Background for War	**6**
The Opposing Commanders	**8**
The French Commanders	8
The German Commanders	9
The Opposing Armies	**13**
Forces Engaged	13
Air Forces	15
Morale	18
The Opposing Plans	**28**
French Strategy	28
German Strategy	29
The Battle for France	**31**
10 May	31
11 May	36
12 May	39
13 May: Over the Meuse	44
14 May	58
15 May: German Exploitation	65
16 May	69
17 May	72
The General Scene: 16 and 17 May	75
18 to 23 May	77
Dunkirk	85
The Result	**88**
Chronology	**92**
A Guide to Further Reading	**93**
Wargaming France 1940	**94**
Index	**97**
Places of Interest	**99**

BACKGROUND FOR WAR

This is one of the classic battles of the twentieth century – a classic in the sense of the almost unique quality of the plan. It was a battle in which practically all the luck went to the attacker; where the greatest army in Europe (as many still thought) was beaten in a matter of days by a well trained, youthful army unleashed in a veritable lightning attack upon its old foe.

But what of France at this time? Divided politically, it was a country that dreaded being launched into war, for the memory of the appalling casualties suffered just twenty years before remained ever present. And, while the French generals could look back to the successes of 1918, they took the easy path of relying upon a policy of

defence, embodied in the so-called Maginot Line. However, the forts extended only halfway along the frontier of France, for they had cost an enormous amount to construct. Too little had been spent on tanks and other heavy equipment that was expensive to manufacture; and the French Air Force too was weak, with many obsolescent aircraft. More often than not, the tendency had been to make do with second best.

Meanwhile, Hitler had restored to German youth its sense of pride. Believing in short wars, he had set about moulding his army to this end, training the young men in aggressive, thrusting tactics, putting the best troops into fully mobile units. Thereby he succeeded in creating a new kind

Adolf Hitler.

of army, testing it and its weapons in combat during the Spanish Civil War.

This account of the Battle of France concentrates on those few days in May 1940 when the panzer divisions sliced into France and, turning westward, cut through to reach the sea. At this point France had lost the battle. Her army had been split in two; her Allies were surrounded; her battle plans had collapsed. It was to be seventeen days before an armistice was signed, but the Battle of France was already over. Despite courageous fighting, the remnants of the French Army were to be swept remorselessly back. Paris would fall to the Germans and much of France was to come under the control of the victor.

Albert Lebrun, President of France, inspecting a British Guard of Honour.

H.M. King George VI visiting the British Expeditionary Force. From left to right: His Majesty, President Lebrun, the French Premier M. Daladier, and General Lord Gort.

THE OPPOSING COMMANDERS

The French Commanders

General Maurice Gamelin was Chief of the General Staff of National Defence for France and, at the outbreak of war, Supreme Commander of all their land forces. In 1914 he had served on Joffre's Operations Staff and by 1916 he had become one of the youngest and most competent divisional commanders. Now he was reaching sixty–eight and had faintly monkish characteristics. He was a small man who usually wore a tight tunic and well–cut breeches with high–laced boots. His headquarters was at Vincennes where he worked with a small staff; cut off from the outside world, there being no radio centre. He had been described as a 'military prefect' who always bore the politicians in mind, and was firmly set in the theories of 1918. As an intellectual he divorced himself from contact with the troops, with whom he felt ill at ease. Indeed the Prime Minister, Reynaud, said of him, 'He might be all right as a prefect or a bishop, but he is not a leader of men.'

Paul Reynaud was a successful barrister who came to power at the age of sixty-two. A small man, dapper with sharp features, he had courage and a sharp intellect and was described as 'a little fighting cock'. Reynaud's personal life, and indeed much of his public life as well, was ruled by his mistress, the Comtesse Hélène de Portes, an ambitious and haughty woman who had her fingers in every pie.

On the left, General Giraud, commanding the French Seventh Army. The other British officer is Lord Gort, in the mackintosh.

Visit of General Ironside and inspection of the French troops. From the left: Generals Ironside, Gamelin, Georges and Lord Gort.

The general who commanded the troops on the North East Front was General Georges. Here was an officer who had risen entirely through professional merit, and who was considered by many to be France's first soldier. He was, however, at loggerheads with Gamelin, with whom he was barely on speaking terms.

No 1 Army Group, which stretched from the northern end of the Maginot Line to the coast, was commanded by General Billotte. He had under him five armies including the British Expeditionary Force, and it is those armies on the right with which we shall be primarily concerned. These were: Second Army, commanded by General Huntziger; Ninth Army, General Corap, and First Army, General Blanchard. Each army had two or three corps, plus some cavalry. Within the corps, the divisions were categorized Regular (R), Fortress (F) and a lower category 'A' or 'B'. Colonel Goutard comments that the regular divisions and those in the 'A' series 'were generally in good shape', but those in the 'B' series 'were very mediocre, and were quite incapable of taking part in a campaign before further training'.

The German Commanders

On the German side Field Marshal Heinrich von Brauchitsch was Commander-in-Chief of the Army, and a man of exceptional intelligence. But he was quiet and highly strung, and although a good soldier he was quite unable to stand up to Hitler.

It is Army Group 'A', and to a lesser extent Group 'B' that concern us – and these were commanded by General von Rundstedt and General von Bock. Von Rundstedt was sixty-four years old and had been called back from retirement to command an army group in the Polish campaign. Now with Army Group 'A' he was to face the Ardennes country of Belgium. His Chief of Staff was von Manstein, twelve years younger than von Rundstedt, extremely outspoken and as a leader commanding respect.

The choice of a leader for the principal group of panzer divisions was selected, probably by Hitler, from those who had commanded in Poland. General Ewald von Kleist was the man, having been brought back from retirement. Von Kleist was typical of the cavalry general, and somewhat old-

General Keitel.

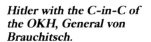

Hitler with the C-in-C of the OKH, General von Brauchitsch.

General von Rundstedt, commanding Army Group 'A' of the German Forces.

fashioned and conservative. In von Kleist's Panzer Corps we find an officer of extensive knowledge and experience in armoured warfare. General Heinz Guderian had been a signals specialist during the Great War and had been Intelligence Officer at the Crown Prince's Headquarters at Verdun in 1916. He later assisted the then Lieutenant-Colonel von Brauchitsch in co-operation between motorized troops and aircraft. His success during these exercises led to his lecturing on tactics and military history. Soon he received command of a battalion equipped with dummy tanks and anti-tank guns – these being all that the army was allowed.

Britain at this time was experimenting with tanks under General Hobart in 1934, and Guderian kept abreast by using, at his own expense,

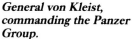

*General von Kleist,
commanding the Panzer
Group.*

*General Guderian,
commanding XIX Panzer
Corps.*

someone to translate all the articles being published in Britain. His book *Achtung! Panzer!* demonstrated the extent of his theories for the breakthrough by armoured forces, supported by aircraft. A force with its own infantry and with strong numbers of anti-tank guns and its own anti-aircraft artillery. A force not relying upon heavy artillery pounding for days to break a line, but upon surprise attack. Everything should be mobile – even the guns should be self-propelled on tracks. His book outlining these theories was ignored by both the French and the British. By 1935 Guderian was General Commanding 2nd Panzer Division and in 1940 he commanded XIX Panzer Corps.

At this point another general who led a panzer division, Erwin Rommel, should be mentioned. In 1940 he was forty-eight years old – a survivor from

the Great War. He had a reputation for strong action as a front-line leader. At Caporetto in 1917 he got through the Italian lines at dawn, and fifty hours later returned with 151 Italian officers, 9,000 men and 81 guns, a feat for which he was promoted captain and received the award of Pour le Mérite. By 1935 he was a lieutenant-colonel at the Potsdam War Academy, and he later commanded the War Academy at Wiener-Neustadt as full colonel. In 1938 he published a textbook on infantry tactics and later during the occupation of the Sudetenland he commanded the battalion guarding Hitler. The following year he was a major-general and again responsible for Hitler's personal safety during the Polish campaign. In February 1940 he was given command of a light division converting to panzers, and in three months he took the division into battle.

THE OPPOSING ARMIES

Forces Engaged

The most westerly point of the Maginot Line was at la Ferté just north of Margut, and it was west of this point, against the North-East Front that Germany struck in May 1940. There were 94 French divisions on this front, but these were of mixed value. In addition there were 22 Belgian divisions, 10 British (some below strength) and 10 Dutch – totalling 136. Hitler could call on 136 out of 157 divisions, of which about one-third were top quality.

The Allies had about 3,000 tanks; the Germans just over 2,400 of mixed quality, not including carriers or armoured cars. The French had a new 33-ton 'B' tank and a fast 20-ton 'Somua'. The 'B' tank had a 47mm gun in a revolving turret and a 75mm gun in the hull; the 'Somua' also had the 47mm high-velocity gun. The total of these two tanks at 800 was greater than the combined total of the German Marks III and IV tanks. Other French tanks were the R35 (Renault) and the H35 (Hotchkiss), both mounting the old-fashioned 37mm gun which was useless against current armour. Certain other factors influenced the deployment of the French tanks. First, four-fifths of them had no radio which was a very serious handicap. Secondly, and more importantly, their crew training and doctrine was vastly inferior to that

A Hotchkiss H-35 tank, with the old-fashioned 37mm gun, being examined by a German soldier.

'Somua', a fast 20-ton tank which mounted a high-velocity 47mm gun.

Renault R-35 French tank, which still mounted the 37mm gun.

Renault R35 of 1st Battalion, 1st Tank Regiment. Illustration by Terry Hadler.

Pz Kpfw II Ausf B of 7th Panzer Regiment, 10 Panzer Division. Illustration by Terry Hadler.

of the German panzer troops. Far worse was the fact that the French tanks were 'lobbed out' among the infantry divisions, some 1,500 to 1,700 of them; while about 700–800 were given to the cavalry divisions or DLMs. The remaining tanks went to the three new armoured divisions being formed in 1940 – each of which had only half the number of tanks of the panzer divisions.

The German Mark II tank with a 20mm canon provided half the strength of the panzer divisions, for there were more than 1,400 Marks I and II. Of the remaining tanks there were 349 medium Mark III with a 37mm gun, and 278 new 24-ton Mark IV with a low-velocity 75mm gun.

In anti-tank guns the French had a superior 47mm, which was in very short supply, and only sixteen divisions had received any. The guns were drawn by converted tractors, but the ammunition was carried in lorries which could not go across country. The 25mm guns were heavy, horse-drawn and also were in short supply. No anti-tank mines had been ordered before the war broke out – and were only just being delivered.

As for artillery the French were far superior to the Germans with 11,200 guns of various sizes, compared with the German total of 7,700. But while both nations used horse transport for their

In addition to the German Mark II tank, the Mark I also played a key role in the Panzer divisions. Shown here is a PzKpfw I Ausf.B, armed with two 7.92mm machine-guns.

artillery, the German panzer divisions had self-propelled guns to keep pace with the tanks.

In anti-aircraft weapons there was a great discrepancy between the French and Germans. The French had only seventeen guns of 90mm; and of the light anti-aircraft guns 22 divisions in the Army each had twelve 20mm guns, while thirteen divisions had six each of the new 25mm guns. Some 39 batteries were kept in reserve; the remainder of the anti-aircraft defence were 75mms, dating from 1918. The Germans, however, had 2,600 of the powerful 88mm gun, plus 6,700 light flak for the panzer and motorized divisions.

Air Forces

It was in the air that Germany dominated. The French total of aircraft was approximately 1,200 with the British adding a further 600, taking account of bombers flying from England. Against

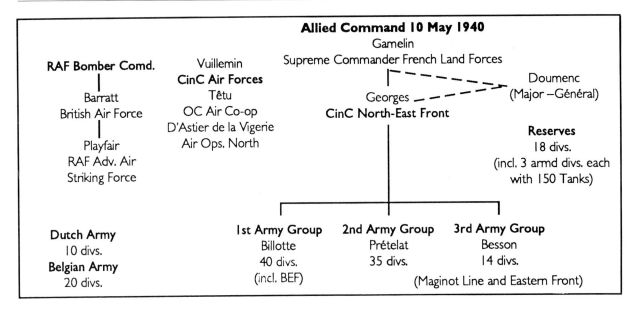

Allied Command 10 May 1940
Gamelin
Supreme Commander French Land Forces

RAF Bomber Comd.	Vuillemin		Doumenc
	CinC Air Forces		(Major –Général)
Barratt	Têtu	Georges	
British Air Force	OC Air Co-op	**CinC North-East Front**	
	D'Astier de la Vigerie		**Reserves**
Playfair	Air Ops. North		18 divs.
RAF Adv. Air			(incl. 3 armd divs. each
Striking Force			with 150 Tanks)

Dutch Army	1st Army Group	2nd Army Group	3rd Army Group
10 divs.	Billotte	Prételat	Besson
Belgian Army	40 divs.	35 divs.	14 divs.
20 divs.	(incl. BEF)		(Maginot Line and Eastern Front)

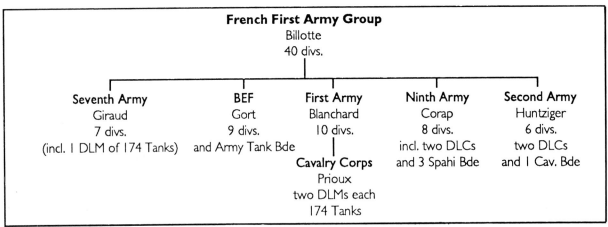

French First Army Group
Billotte
40 divs.

Seventh Army	BEF	First Army	Ninth Army	Second Army
Giraud	Gort	Blanchard	Corap	Huntziger
7 divs.	9 divs.	10 divs.	8 divs.	6 divs.
(incl. 1 DLM of 174 Tanks)	and Army Tank Bde		incl. two DLCs	two DLCs
		Cavalry Corps	and 3 Spahi Bde	and 1 Cav. Bde
		Prioux		
		two DLMs each		
		174 Tanks		

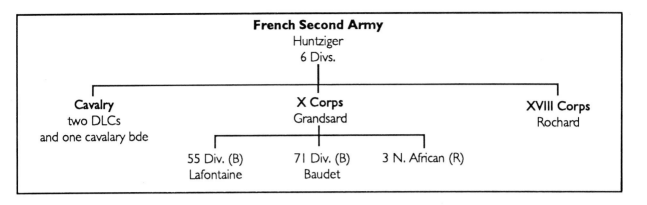

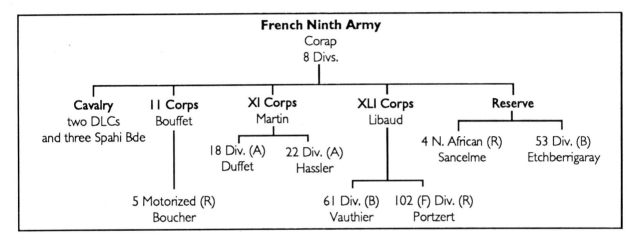

this Goering could deploy 3,000–3,500 aircraft, not counting a number of Ju 52 transport aircraft. Standard air transport aircraft did not exist in the French air force, which brought great problems over mobility. France was also short of bombers, having only 150–175, and few had any radio. Regarding fighter aircraft, their Morane 406 was 50mph slower than the German Me 109 and mostly were without any radio. There were few Moranes and the balance was made up of Bloch and the outclassed Dewoitine and some larger aircraft – the Potez 63. The British Royal Air Force in France had about 130 Hurricane fighters.

The standard German bomber was the Ju 88 with a top speed of 300mph, and the standard fighter was the Me 109, which had a top speed of 350mph and battle endurance of one hour. While the French had only 50 dive-bombers, the

On the right, RAF Fairey Battle bomber, and on the left a French Morane fighter.

Germans put into the field some 342 Stuka Ju 87s. This aircraft had emerged in 1935 and was adopted the following autumn. Single-engined with a fixed undercarriage and a crew of two, it was armed with three machine-guns and a bomb load of 1,000lb. With a top speed of 200mph and a radius of action of 100 miles, it had the attribute that its bombs could be placed with great accuracy. Being vulnerable to anti-aircraft fire it was equipped with a siren which howled when diving, intended to demoralize the ground troops being attacked. Its greatest asset was the fact that it could be used as 'mobile artillery' for attacking any target behind the battlefront swiftly, and was quite devastating.

As for reconnaissance aircraft, these were fairly well balanced between the Germans and the French, but the Ju 52 transport aircraft had no parallel in France and gave the Germans the advantage of being able to supply their aircraft and panzer divisions with ammunition and fuel and all else urgently needed as they moved forward. Above all, the Luftwaffe had taken the golden opportunity

Messerschmitt Bf 109E-1 of 2/JG27, early 1940. (Illustration by Terry Hadler)

German Junkers Ju 87 dive-bomber or 'Stuka', not showing the bombs, which would be attached under the wings and fuselage. It had a 2-man crew, and when it dived on the target it emitted a screeching whistle.

of fighting in Spain and Portugal during the Civil War, and much experience had been gained.

Morale

When war broke out in 1939, France came reluctantly into a war that she had dreaded since the end of the Great War. The appalling casualties that had left a scar on every family in France could not be forgotten. When Mobilization was called there was no hysteria in France, or indeed in Berlin or London. There were too many remembering what had happened twenty-odd years previously. France indeed was in a tough spot with an army that was weak and an air-force that was outclassed. Furthermore the nation was divided politically and socially, a situation that led to frequent changes in government.

German propaganda also played its part. For instance in 1938 General Vuillemin, Chief of French Air Staff, visited Heinkel's Oranienburg works in Germany. Here Heinkel and others did all they could to impress their visitor. Taking him up in an experimental He 100, he was told that the model was already in full production, when in fact only three prototypes existed. Then he was taken to workshops where He 111 bombers were in mass production. General Vuillemin's reaction made a profound impression of the Luftwaffe's strength upon the French. In any case by 1939 Germany was producing up to 3,000 aircraft annually, while France could only produce 600 a year.

When the war came the French were saying 'Let's get it over with!' Within ten days doubts had spread, and after the twentieth day the comment was 'la drôle de guerre' an expression that became in the United States 'phoney war'. At the front, among the many divisions lining the long frontier, the enemy soon became 'pas méchants' – an idea fostered by the Germans. The ordinary soldier often had a good deal to put up with. For instance in the Second Army on the Sedan front, there were no proper billets and the men slept in the stables with their horses. Their officers, ignoring the orders to wear helmet, gas mask and belt on active service, were often seen strolling about wearing service caps and jackets unbuttoned, an attitude which intentionally distanced them from their men. Soon the army became tainted with that pernicious disease – boredom. Soldiers started to take 'French leave', slipping off at the weekend, often not getting back until Monday morning.

Almost more serious, however, was the influence of the Communist Party, which turned against the government. Here the German propaganda machine under Goebbels could find friends and took full advantage. One of the targets was the British; why was the British soldier paid 17 francs a day, when the French *poilu* only got fifty centimes? It was the British who had dragged France into the war, and now only sent ten divisions! And so on. Alistair Horne describes acts of sabotage by Communists working in factories manufacturing war material. One of these took

French infantryman. Illustration by Richard Geiger.

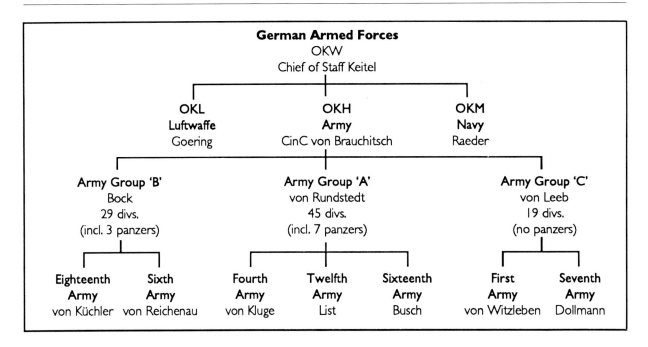

German Armed Forces
OKW
Chief of Staff Keitel

OKL	**OKH**	**OKM**
Luftwaffe	Army	Navy
Goering	CinC von Brauchitsch	Raeder

Army Group 'B'	**Army Group 'A'**	**Army Group 'C'**
Bock	von Rundstedt	von Leeb
29 divs.	45 divs.	19 divs.
(incl. 3 panzers)	(incl. 7 panzers)	(no panzers)

Eighteenth Army	Sixth Army	Fourth Army	Twelfth Army	Sixteenth Army	First Army	Seventh Army
von Küchler	von Reichenau	von Kluge	List	Busch	von Witzleben	Dollmann

Above and left: German heavy artillery in action.

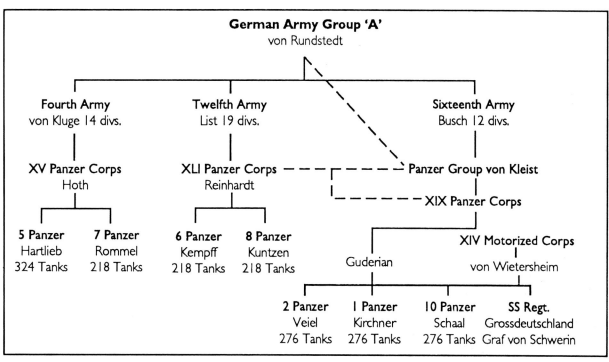

German Army Group 'A'
von Rundstedt

Fourth Army	Twelfth Army	Sixteenth Army
von Kluge 14 divs.	List 19 divs.	Busch 12 divs.

XV Panzer Corps — Hoth

XLI Panzer Corps — Reinhardt

Panzer Group von Kleist

XIX Panzer Corps

5 Panzer	7 Panzer	6 Panzer	8 Panzer
Hartlieb	Rommel	Kempff	Kuntzen
324 Tanks	218 Tanks	218 Tanks	218 Tanks

Guderian

XIV Motorized Corps
von Wietersheim

2 Panzer	1 Panzer	10 Panzer	SS Regt.
Veiel	Kirchner	Schaal	Grossdeutschland
276 Tanks	276 Tanks	276 Tanks	Graf von Schwerin

Messerschmitt Bf 109E-1
of Staffelkapitän, 2/JG27.
Illustration by Terry
Hadler.

STRUCTURE OF A

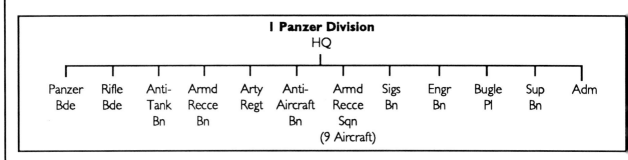

1 Panzer Division
HQ

| Panzer Bde | Rifle Bde | Anti-Tank Bn | Armd Recce Bn | Arty Regt | Anti-Aircraft Bn | Armd Recce Sqn (9 Aircraft) | Sigs Bn | Engr Bn | Bugle Pl | Sup Bn | Adm |

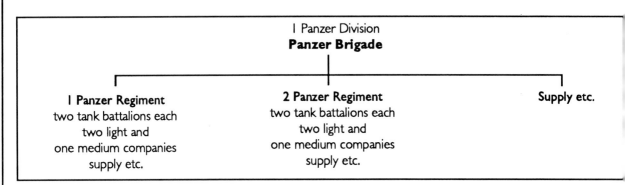

1 Panzer Division
Panzer Brigade

1 Panzer Regiment
two tank battalions each
two light and
one medium companies
supply etc.

2 Panzer Regiment
two tank battalions each
two light and
one medium companies
supply etc.

Supply etc.

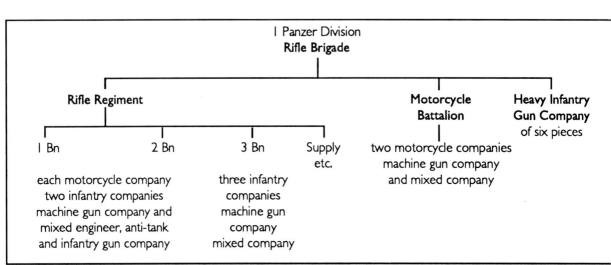

1 Panzer Division
Rifle Brigade

Rifle Regiment

1 Bn

each motorcycle company
two infantry companies
machine gun company and
mixed engineer, anti-tank
and infantry gun company

2 Bn

3 Bn

three infantry
companies
machine gun
company
mixed company

Supply
etc.

Motorcycle
Battalion

two motorcycle companies
machine gun company
and mixed company

Heavy Infantry
Gun Company
of six pieces

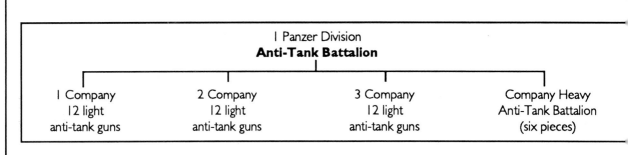

1 Panzer Division
Anti-Tank Battalion

| 1 Company 12 light anti-tank guns | 2 Company 12 light anti-tank guns | 3 Company 12 light anti-tank guns | Company Heavy Anti-Tank Battalion (six pieces) |

PANZER DIVISION

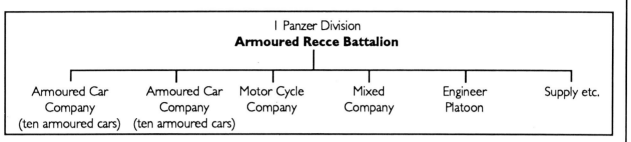

I Panzer Division
Armoured Recce Battalion

| Armoured Car Company (ten armoured cars) | Armoured Car Company (ten armoured cars) | Motor Cycle Company | Mixed Company | Engineer Platoon | Supply etc. |

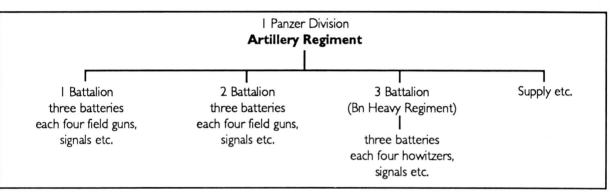

I Panzer Division
Artillery Regiment

I Battalion
three batteries
each four field guns,
signals etc.

2 Battalion
three batteries
each four field guns,
signals etc.

3 Battalion
(Bn Heavy Regiment)

three batteries
each four howitzers,
signals etc.

Supply etc.

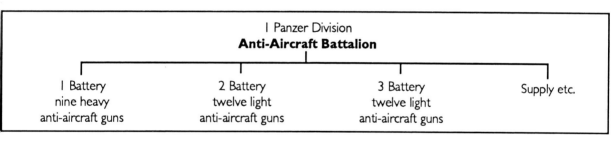

I Panzer Division
Anti-Aircraft Battalion

I Battery
nine heavy
anti-aircraft guns

2 Battery
twelve light
anti-aircraft guns

3 Battery
twelve light
anti-aircraft guns

Supply etc.

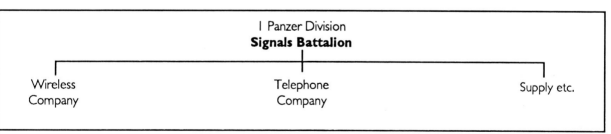

I Panzer Division
Signals Battalion

Wireless
Company

Telephone
Company

Supply etc.

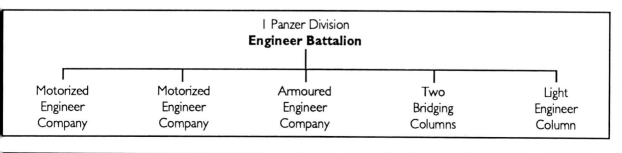

I Panzer Division
Engineer Battalion

Motorized
Engineer
Company

Motorized
Engineer
Company

Armoured
Engineer
Company

Two
Bridging
Columns

Light
Engineer
Column

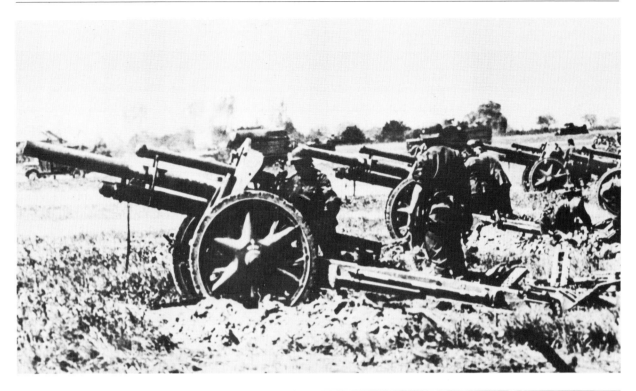

Above left: German 10.5cm artillery; below left, French 75mm guns on parade.

place in the Renault tank works in Paris. A report on the damage wreaked upon Renault's production of the B1, France's gravely needed new heavy tank, itemized: '...nuts, bolts, various bits of old iron put into gear boxes and transmissions...filings and emery dust in the crank cases; saw-strokes producing incipient rupture of the oil and petrol ducts, intended to make them fall to bits after several hours running...' In April 1940 a number of fatal flying accidents led investigators to the Farman factory. Here it was found that on engines ready for delivery a brass wire acting as a lock to hold the petrol fuel nozzle in position had been severed. After a number of hours' flying, the nut unscrewed itself with the engine vibration and allowed the petrol to drip on to the white hot exhaust pipe which eventually led to a lethal explosion! A young Communist was caught in the act, having stripped off the locking wires of seventeen out of twenty engines on the test bed.

In Germany there were also many who thought back to their suffering during the Great War, and there was certainly little enthusiasm for the war. Rationing had been observed since the start and had cut food consumption to some 75 per cent, but nobody went hungry. Nor had the Allies attacked in eight months and, particularly after the Norwegian campaign when everything had gone well for Germany, the population began to relax a little. The young believed implicitly in Hitler and his successes, unlike some of his senior generals who resented his methods and were nervous of his certainty. Nevertheless, Hitler had created a superlative war machine. Of the support of Nazism, a German who survived the war said recently: 'Five per cent of Germans were good, and five per cent were evil. The remainder was 90 per cent, and they were not particularly good or particularly evil, they just accepted Nazism and went along with it.'

Pz Kpfw II Ausf C of 4 Panzer Division. Illustration by Terry Hadler.

THE OPPOSING PLANS

French Strategy

Gamelin was an officer who had survived the Great War, but seemed incapable of grasping any of the lessons learned since then. His strategy was to wait until Britain and France could reach at least parity with Germany before taking any serious offensive. This could not happen until 1941 – when perhaps America might intervene. Otherwise the principal considerations were the same as they had been since 1919 – no repetition of the slaughter experienced in the Great War, and to keep the war away from the sacred soil of France. But if Hitler did not wait – what then? He might attack across the frontier, going direct for Paris; or go through Belgium, at present neutral. This seemed the plan that Hitler would find his best bet. King Leopold of Belgium anyway would not even discuss contingency plans and Holland was also neutral.

However, while the arguments flowed back and forth, an incident occurred that could have had very dramatic results. On 10 January 1940 a German major of paratroops was flying to Cologne with a friend in a small Me 108. Hellmuth Reinberger had to take top-secret documents to a secret conference at the German Second Air Fleet Headquarters. The plans related to the air plan for invading Holland and Belgium. Suddenly the weather closed in, and the pilot, realizing that he had strayed off

Churchill, then First Lord of the Admiralty, conferring with General Lord Gort at his headquarters at the beginning of the war.

Hitler makes plans. From the left: Goering, General Bodenschatz, General Keitel, Hitler and von Ribbentrop.

course, started to change direction, when the engine suddenly failed. He managed to land on a snow-covered field, which was inside Belgian territory. Reinberger tried to burn the vital documents behind a hedge. Soon both men were arrested and taken to a Belgian post. Here Reinberger again tried to destroy the remaining documents by thrusting them into a stove. By nightfall the remaining papers were in the hands of Belgian GHQ and there was sufficient evidence of Germany's intention to invade northern France via Belgium and Holland. The effect on Gamelin was to convince him of the German intention to carry out a second Schlieffen Plan of 1914. But Belgium remained tenaciously neutral.

In March, Gamelin instituted the Dyle–Breda Plan. On the left was General Giraud's strong Seventh Army. Next came the BEF under Lord Gort who were to advance up to the River Dyle between Louvain and Wavre: then General Blanchard's First Army, holding the Gembloux Gap down to Namur on the Meuse: while General Corap's Ninth Army was to wheel forward to occupy the line of the Meuse to just north of Sedan. At this point was placed General Huntziger's Second Army down to the start of the Maginot Line at Longwy. Both these two divisions were mediocre: the best divisions and the majority of the armour were placed to counter the Germans in the north and to help Holland. The approach through the Ardennes was regarded by the French High Command as 'impenetrable' to a modern army. If any attack were made from this direction it would have to be supported by heavy artillery, which would take a long time to assemble in such country, and this should give the French plenty of time to bring up reserves.

German Strategy

The evolution of the final plan for invading France went through many stages and brought forward some of the finest professional men of modern warfare. Much of the early work was done by von

Manstein, who had the active support of Field Marshal von Rundstedt, and it was von Manstein who was eventually secretly called for by Hitler to present the plan in detail. Delighted that it followed so closely some of his own ideas, Hitler took it over and within a few days it was issued by General Halder, the Chief of Staff for OKH. So Operation 'Sichelschnitt' (the cut of the sickle) was born.

The concept was bold, simple and admirably suited to the new ideas of armoured warfare. In the north General von Bock's Army Group 'B' (29 divisions, including some panzers) would draw the French and British up to their stop line, and hold them so vigorously that they could not break away to attack the flank of von Rundstedt's thrust. Army Group 'A', under Field Marshal von Rundstedt, had its northern boundary south of Liège and consisted of three Armies: Fourth, Twelfth and Sixteenth, with a total of 45 divisions. Army Group 'C' had the First and Seventh Armies deployed from Luxemburg to the Swiss frontier. Seven Panzer divisions were concentrated under command of General von Kleist and would advance through the 'impenetrable' Ardennes country to breach the Meuse between Dinant and Sedan with the main thrust by Guderian's XIX Panzer Corps of 1, 2 and 10 Panzer Divisions, the élite Regiment Grossdeutschland and von Wietersheim's XIV Motorized Corps. Further north the 6 and 8 Panzer Divisions would make for Monthermé, and 5 and 7 Panzers would cross the Meuse at Dinant.

Some refinements had been added by Hitler. Most of the heavier Mark III and IV tanks were withdrawn from von Küchler's Eighteenth Army and given to von Kleist and von Rundstedt where the guns could be used to silence the bunkers on the banks of the Meuse. Also certain 'special operations' would secure key bridges on the Dutch and Belgian canals. Finally, in an attempt to hold down the reserves in that area, deception plans would be put into operation to convince the French that an attack on the Maginot Line would take place.

Meanwhile in the Eifel Mountains the panzer divisions were busy preparing their vehicles and tanks; always ready to move at twenty-four hours' notice. Day by day with exercises of all kinds, the problems were ironed out, as the men worked hard at bringing themselves and their weapons to an ever higher pitch of efficiency.

Pz Kpfw I Ausf B of 4 Panzer Division. Illustration by Terry Hadler.

THE BATTLE FOR FRANCE

10 May

The previous day the orders had gone out, and at 0430 hours on 10 May the leading panzers crossed the Luxemburg frontier. But these were not the first Germans to enter Luxemburg; for several days a number of 'tourists' on bicycles and motor-cycles had crossed and now occupied vital road junctions. Further north, German stormtroopers waited, hidden close to the Customs Houses. As dawn broke a rumbling was heard growing louder and louder as squadrons of Ju 52s with the German 22 Airborne Division of some 4,000 paratroops passed overhead. The Luftwaffe bomber crews had been turned out of their beds for briefing at fifteen minutes' notice and took off at first light. Their objectives were far and wide – laying mines in the Channel, attacking airfields in Holland, Belgium and France, and road and railway centres deep into France. The RAF lost six Blenheims and twelve were damaged at their airfield at Condé-sur-Marne, near Vraux. Nearly fifty of the French airfields were attacked, but General d'Astier's report was modest – four aircraft destroyed and thirty damaged.

It was against Holland that the full fury of the Luftwaffe was aimed, with fighters machine-gunning the streets of The Hague and bombers concentrating on the airfields where the Dutch Air Force was concentrated. Behind came the paratroops of the airborne division. Here was the

The triple-engined Ju 52, Germany's equivalent of the Dakota, an invaluable cargo-carrying aircraft.

strength of the Luftwaffe visible for all to see – but watching over the panzers packed along the roads from the Eifel into the Ardennes was constant fighter cover to prevent any Allied 'spy' aircraft observing the great concentration of tanks. Behind came motorized infantry, then the heavy supply vehicles and finally the marching infantry regiments whose job would be to consolidate the ground captured by the panzers. The phalanx of vehicles and troops stretched back a hundred miles.

In Belgium, guarding Liège and the Albert Canal was a modern fortification, Eben Emael, built in 1935, bristling with artillery and garrisoned by a battalion of infantry. Curiously it possessed very little anti-aircraft defence, certainly nothing on the roof. The task of neutralizing this fortification was given to a team of German volunteer sappers

The 'top brass' of the Allied armies inspecting a British 8in howitzer.

who had been training secretly since November 1939. In the dark, early on 10 May, they took off in eleven large gliders each carrying seven or eight men and towed by a Ju 52. Despite an early disaster, when two of the tow ropes snapped (one of the gliders carried the Commander, Lieutenant Witzig) the other gliders landed safely, some on top of the fort. Here Sergeant-Major Wenzel took charge, and the engineers systematically blasted the steel covers to the gun turrets, using powerful hollow charges, a method used for the first time. By the time Lieutenant Witzig arrived the teeth of the fort had been drawn and he set about the garrison inside, but it was not until the next day that the advance troops of von Reichenau's Sixth Army arrived and Eben Emael surrendered. Captain

A German parachute regiment recruit photographed in his new uniform.

Koch, who trained the team, and Lieutenant Witzig both received the Ritterkreuz, one of Germany's highest decorations. Meanwhile Goebbels' propaganda machine made much of the 'new method of attack', never mentioning the true reasons for the success, which produced many dark rumours among the Allies.

In France General Gamelin gave the order for the Dyle-Breda Plan to start at 0700 on 10 May and then drafted his Order of the Day. It was all

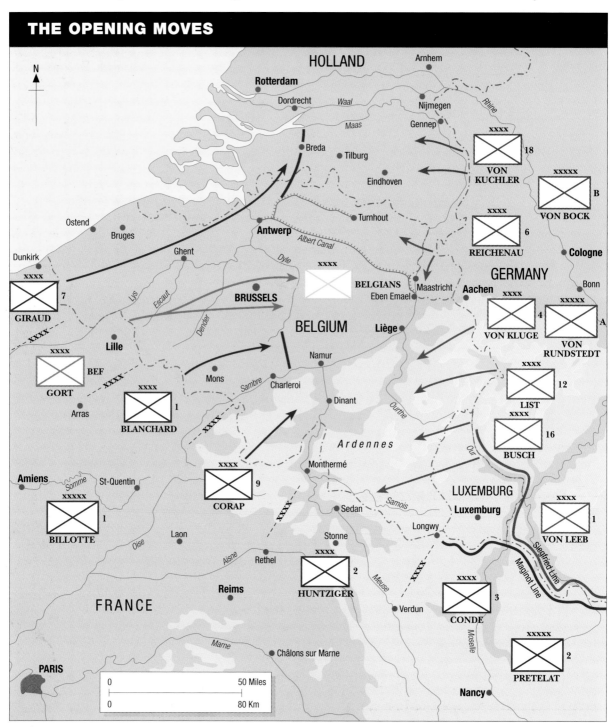

THE OPENING MOVES

happening, he thought, as he had imagined it would.

In the south, the commander of France's Ninth Army was General Corap. A Norman, he was sixty-two and had spent most of his career in North Africa where, in 1926, he had captured the famous rebel Abel-el-Krim. He was a portly man and was well liked by his troops, but his military education had ended in 1918.

General Huntziger, who commanded Second Army, was half-Breton and half-Alsatian and was regarded as a brilliant intellect. He had fought in the pre-1914 colonial wars in Madagascar and Indo-China, commanded a battalion in the Great War and later the French forces in Syria before being appointed to the Conseil Supérieur de la Guerre in 1938. Still under sixty and with a youthful figure, he was regarded as a successor to Gamelin. Unfortunately he had the same flaw, an inability to think beyond the firm belief in a rigid linear defence.

On Corap's front the infantry divisions marched forward to the Meuse and the cavalry

French anti-aircraft gun in camouflaged pit, near Mesnil.

French heavy AA gun, left over from 1918

went ahead into the Ardennes. The infantry advance went less smoothly. General Martin's XI Corps had a number of battalions on exercises, while 18 Division had fifty-five miles to go to reach Dinant, and could only rush up two battalions by truck on 10 May. The remainder would be there on 14 May; but they considered the Germans could not reach the river until the 16th. The bunkers that they were leaving were to be locked and the keys handed to 53 Division – which in fact was moved south, so the bunkers remained locked.

On General Huntziger's front the 2 DLC came up against Guderian's left-hand panzer division about eight miles north-west of Arlon at 0900 hours on 10 May. Confused fighting took place, but the cavalry was forced back on the River Semois in the afternoon. A similar engagement took place near Esch, but that evening the French pulled back, their withdrawal much hampered by some 25,000 civilians trying to flee down the only road to the French frontier. On the left of Huntziger's front 5 DLC covered the open country Neufchâteau–Libramont–Bastogne through which Guderian's main body was advancing, but had been delayed by

Belgian demolitions. On that evening of 10 May, the Belgian Chasseurs Ardennais moved northwards according to their orders, except for part of the 3rd Regiment who fought off Rommel's motorcycle battalion and prevented his getting to the River Ourthe that night.

Allied air attacks on 10 May were seriously limited by Gamelin's veto on bombing any built-up areas; he was terrified of the threat of Luftwaffe reprisals. He had at any rate limited action to 'fighters and reconnaissance' and only later amended this to allow the bombing of enemy columns with airfields as second priority, but avoiding built-up areas. In desperation Barratt sent off a flight of Fairey Battles to attack columns advancing through Luxemburg. They were met by a torrent of anti-aircraft fire and attacked by Me 109s. Of the thirty-two dispatched on 10 May, thirteen were lost and all the rest damaged.

11 May

In the north, 5 and 7 Panzer Divisions were marching on Dinant, while von Kleist's Panzer

A flight of Fairey Battles flying with French fighters.

German infantry on the approach march.

Air Marshal Barratt, commanding the British Air Forces in France.

Group was more concentrated; 6 and 8 Panzer Divisions towards Monthermé and Nouzonville, with Guderian's three Panzer Divisions, 2, 1 and 10, advancing on Sedan. First we should follow Fifth and Seventh Armies, for it was Rommel's Panzer Division that was the first over the Meuse; 5 Panzer Division was on the right and from the start had great difficulty moving through the Ardennes and, tangled up on the roads, began to lag behind. Rommel, however, had trained his men well. The engineers seemed to be everywhere and quickly got bridges erected and demolitions removed to get the tanks through. As for the French cavalry, his orders were 'fire first' for he had quickly discovered that 'the day goes to the side that is the first to plaster its opponent with fire'.

Reinhardt's Corps of 6 and 8 Panzer Divisions had set off behind Guderian, and 6 Panzer found its route blocked by elements of 2 Panzer. Again the mechanized engineers worked wonders, replacing bridges and removing road-blocks and constructing road detours. On Guderian's front 1 Panzer broke through the French 5 DLC and surrounded a battery of 105mm field guns. The

British infantryman. Illustration by Richard Geiger

general commanding 5 DLC eventually drew the cavalry back over the Semois, although Huntziger had ordered that it be held at all costs, and had deployed a battalion of 295th Infantry Regiment (from Grandsard's 'B' 55 Division at Sedan) to stiffen the line. To the left of 5 DLC was 3 Spahi Brigade and this too followed the DLC across the Semois. This pretty trout stream was in many places shallow enough to wade across and hardly a natural obstacle. The obvious route was through Bouillon, but here the ground was easier to defend. By nightfall, 1 Panzer reached the outskirts of Bouillon and, finding the bridges destroyed, pulled back, it being decided to attack with the motorized infantry the next day.

In the air, the Luftwaffe was careful not to place too much effort over the Ardennes, but continued to annihilate Dutch resistance in the north. A squadron of Belgian Battles was sent off to bomb the bridges over the Maastricht and the Albert Canal bridges – ten out of fifteen aircraft were lost. Then the RAF Blenheims were sent on the same mission, but five out of six were brought down by flak. In desperation Gamelin got in touch with d'Astier, ordering him to 'put everything to work to slow up the German columns in the direction of Maastricht, Tongeren, Gembloux', including orders to bomb any built-up areas needed to get this result. But time had been irredeemably lost – and the limited effort was in the wrong place!

Meanwhile the BEF had reached its positions on the Dyle and was dug-in on a relatively strong position. General Blanchard's forced-marching to fill the 'Gembloux Gap' had serious problems. News came of the fall of Eben Emael; and the German advance had been so rapid that General Prioux with the Cavalry Corps reported that it would be almost impossible to complete the 'Dyle Manoeuvre'. Billotte was horrified and, having visited Prioux that night, ordered him to hold fast until 14 May. In Holland matters were even worse. The air force had been almost wiped out and the Dutch Army had been forced back on Rotterdam. General Giraud's Seventh Army had run into 9 Panzer Division near Tilburg, and his tank units had given way and retired towards Antwerp, followed up by the low-flying Luftwaffe. All this activity kept Gamelin's eyes rooted on the situation in the north, although it would not be true to say that there were no reports of the danger of an attack through the Ardennes. As d'Astier had said in his midday bulletin on 11 May, 'The enemy seems to be preparing an energetic action in the direction of Givet.'

However, the German 'umbrella' against intruders and the natural camouflage of the forests prevented an accurate assessment of the true strength of the German advance through the Ardennes, while General Bock's brandishing of the 'matador's cloak' in the north suggested that much more than a quarter of the panzer strength was deployed there. Nevertheless, General Georges made provisions to move to the second position behind Sedan 2 and 3 Armoured Divisions, 3 Motorized and 14, 36 and 87 Infantry Divisions from the general reserve. Orders for the move would be passed between 11 and 13 May. Events, however, were to prove that they would come too late.

12 May

In Holland the situation was already desperate. The shore of the Zuyder Zee was reached by the Germans, while the Grebbe Line at Rhenen was pierced, and further south 9 Panzer was linking up with the paratroops holding the bridge at Moerdijk. The Dutch Army was forced back to cover the cities of Rotterdam, Amsterdam and Utrecht. In the air the Dutch were reduced to a single bomber, which was shot down the following day. Giraud's armoured units, reduced by losses and with replacements still moving up on the railways, were increasingly menaced by 9 Panzer Division and the ever-present Luftwaffe. Meanwhile Blanchard's troops were ordered to speed-up their advance, but moving by day they came under constant attack by the Luftwaffe. The Belgian Army's withdrawal to link with the BEF exposed Prioux's corps to attack by the panzer corps. The French tanks still held on and the fighting was indecisive, but by nightfall only two-thirds of First Army had reached the Dyle.

The French bombers were not yet ready, and d'Astier had to ask the RAF to attack the Maastricht bridges, but seven out of the nine Blenheims were shot down.. Then at noon Groupe

French infantry on the march.

French horse-drawn artillery moving up slowly.

Two vehicles of a French motorized unit before an attack.

The German Messerschmitt fighter. An Me 109 single-seater fighter aircraft. Top speed 350mph.

A pair of Renault tanks on the edge of a wood. The tank with a flag is the one used by the squadron commander.

1/54 was finally ready. One flight of six Breguets was attacking near Liège when they found an unbelievable target: 'Hundreds and hundreds of vehicles rolling towards France, following each other at short intervals, mobile, and travelling fast.' As the flight attacked, an absolute curtain of flak ripped into the aircraft. Of the six aircraft, one returned – limping down into a field, a write-off; of the Groupe, 50 per cent were lost.

Indeed, the daily tally of Allied air effort in the north was a sorry tale. The RAF bombers made 140 sorties and lost twenty-four; the French thirty sorties losing nine. French fighters flew 200 sorties, lost six aircraft and claimed 26. The German Fighter Group flew 340 sorties, lost four and claimed 28. Again d'Astier reported 'considerable motorized and armoured forces... towards the Meuse round Dinant, Givet and Bouillon', and ended, 'One can assume a very serious enemy effort in the direction of the Meuse.' Much to the astonishment of Billotte, General Georges gave first priority of air support on call to Huntziger, but throughout the remainder of the day the commander of Second Army made no demand for air cover. D'Astier, however, on his own initiative requested the RAF to send fifty aircraft to bomb Neufchâteau and Bouillon that evening. Eighteen failed to return.

DINANT

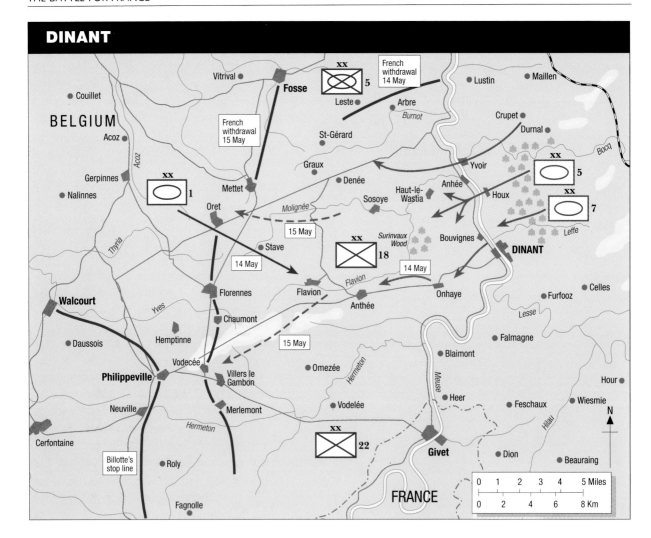

Couillet

BELGIUM

Acoz

Gerpinnes

Nalinnes

Vitrival

Fosse

XX 5

Leste

French withdrawal 14 May

Lustin

Maillen

Arbre

Burnot

St-Gérard

Crupet

Durnal

Bocq

French withdrawal 15 May

XX 1

Mettet

Oret

Graux

Denée

Sosoye

Molignée

Haut-le-Wastia

Yvoir

Anhée

Houx

XX 5

XX 7

Leffe

Stave

15 May

14 May

XX 18

Surinvaux Wood

Bouvignes

DINANT

Thyria

Walcourt

Yves

Florennes

Chaumont

Hemptinne

Daussois

Vodecée

Philippeville

Neuville

Cerfontaine

Billotte's stop line

Villers le Gambon

Merlemont

Hermeton

Roly

Fagnolle

Flavion

Flavion

Anthée

14 May

Onhaye

Furfooz

Celles

Lesse

15 May

Omezée

Hermeton

Vodelée

Blaimont

Meuse

Heer

Falmagne

Hour

Feschaux

Wiesmie

Hilau

XX 22

Givet

Dion

Beauraing

FRANCE

N

0 1 2 3 4 5 Miles

0 2 4 6 8 Km

At noon on 12 May, Rommel had a stroke of luck. He had only one tank regiment, having been converted from a 'light' division. The 31st Panzer Regiment, commanded by Colonel Werner, was the leading regiment of 5 Panzer Division and was transferred temporarily to Rommel's command. After some sharp fighting with the French cavalry rearguard, it pressed on to the River Meuse at Yvoir in the late afternoon. As the French vehicles were crossing, Werner's armoured cars tried to rush the bridge. Lieutenant de Wispelaere of the Belgian Army pressed the demolition plunger – but it failed to explode the charges. At this moment the leading armoured car was stopped by a shell from an anti-tank gun; when the commander ran forward to disconnect the charges he was killed. Meanwhile a second armoured car was halted on the bridge, while de Wispelaere raced forward to detonate the charge by hand. Turning to run back, he was shot down; but with a tremendous explosion the bridge went up, armoured cars and all.

Now the motorized infantry brigade moved up and established control of the east bank of the river. Owing to the lateness of the evening, little reconnaissance had been possible, but at Houx there appeared to be an old weir connected with a narrow island in midstream. It did not seem to be defended, and during the night Rommel's foot patrols reconnoitered the river and found it unguarded. Immediately the motorcycle battalion was ordered forward to attempt a crossing. The men crept forward, groping in the darkness, and made their way to '... the thin spine with many gaps in it which comprises the old, unprotected and weather-worn stone weir'. Machine-guns were placed to give covering fire and very cautiously the first men moved forward balancing precariously. They moved through the scrub on the island and on the far side discovered a lockgate. Covered by their machine-guns they crept forward and dug themselves in. Slowly more and more men crossed and in the noise of the firing several companies succeeded in crossing. Rommel's casualties that day were three officers and twenty-one other ranks, and his division was established across the Meuse,

French troops leading their horses along a woodland path.

albeit precariously. Evidently the French had hesitated to destroy the weir, as the season had been very dry and the river level might have been lowered so much that it became fordable in places. But no special defensive measures had been taken to cover this potentially vulnerable area.

In this area the French were somewhat in disarray, it being on the boundary between General Bouffet's II Corps and General Martin's XI Corps. The French 5 Motorized Division was more or less in position on 12 May, but 18 Division (an 'A' class unit) had only six battalions and some of its artillery in position. The men were exhausted after their march of fifty miles from the frontier. Being very thin on the ground, Martin had borrowed a battalion from 5 Motorized Division to bolster his line. But although 2/39th Regiment received its orders on 11 May, it did not reach its positions until the afternoon of the 12th and was just taking over from 66th Regiment. Knowing that Rommel's men were on the east bank, 39th Regiment took positions on the high ground overlooking the Isle of Haux in complete disregard of Corap's orders to defend the water's edge. While Boucher learned that the Germans had crossed by 0100 on 13 May, Martin did not get the news until 0400 hrs, and then was unable to report the news to Corap.

Reinhardt's sector remained confused and was making very slow progress owing to the jumble of troops on the few routes forward. Nevertheless 6 Panzer Division reported no air attacks and no action by the French on the ground all day. By evening the divisions were approaching the edge of the escarpment overlooking the Meuse. The reason was simply that the withdrawal of 3 Spahi Brigade had left the cavalry exposed. General Corap had ordered the Spahis to re-occupy their positions on the Semois, but the panzers were already across so the entire cavalry screen had to be pulled back to the west side of the Meuse. Instead of holding out for the estimated five days they were all withdrawn in half the time.

Here we must return to the main panzer thrust. Overnight, Guderian had taken advantage of the Spahi withdrawal from the Semois. The motorcyclists of 1 Panzer Division had got across in darkness, and by 0600 on 12 May Guderian had his tanks across at Mouzaive. At Bouillon his Rifle

Regiment forded the river and soon took their objectives. By midday 1 Panzer Division was on the road to Sedan and could see in the distance the heights on the other side of the Meuse. General Huntziger had ordered 5 DLC to fall back on the *maisons fortes* that had been constructed between Sedan and the frontier. But in the early afternoon 1 Panzer's advance had forced them back on the bridgehead at Sedan. The infantry battalion of the 295th Regiment had been even more unlucky – they had broken and run, and 'only three hundred demoralized men were seen again, crying "treachery" against the cavalry and devoid of any value for the actions of the following day'. Meanwhile, 1 Panzer Division pursued the cavalry and by nightfall had forced them to evacuate the major part of Sedan on the east bank of the river. Now as the German infantry and engineers worked their way through the empty streets, heavy artillery shells began to fall, and in turn all the bridges were blown.

Meanwhile, during General Georges' absence from his headquarters, his Chief of Staff received alarming news at 1500 on 12 May that the cavalry had suffered 'very serious losses' and Huntziger was requesting a fresh division to put into the line south of Sedan to replace 71 Division. He ordered three reserve divisions – 3 Armoured, 3 Motorized and 14 Infantry – to move forward. Then at 1700 hours Huntziger's Chief of Staff telephoned to say that 'calm had returned from the front'. But Georges' Chief of Staff stuck to his decision to order 3 Motorized Division to arrive at Sedan on 14 May.

As nightfall came it was evident that the German attack would hit French Second Army the next day. Not only could the noise of the enemy tanks be heard in increasing volume as the night progressed, but reconnaissance air reports gave news of long columns of vehicles moving on all the roads out of the Ardennes, their headlamps blazing in flagrant contempt of the Allied air forces. But what did Huntziger assume would happen? He knew that the French Army could not have made such a crossing before 18 May – and therefore the Germans would do no better, which would give him time to make adjustments and bring up reserves to halt them on the line of the river. 71 Division,

ordered back into position on 10 May, was straggling in, having marched some forty miles in two short nights. Its commander, General Baudet, found that his command post had not been set up and the divisional telephone exchange had hardly been started. Meanwhile General Lafontaine's 55 Division was reorganizing itself to make room for 71 Division, and was planning to complete this by the night of 13/14 May. As for artillery, Grandsard had received two additional regiments, ordered up on 12 May, and with some 140 guns had twice the normal amount of artillery. But much of it was not dug in, and some batteries had not yet arrived. The commander of the 155mm regiment, which had been shelling the Bouillon positions so effectively, had run out of ammunition and withdrawn the regiment, and Grandsard was unable to harass the German approach routes.

The die, however, had already been cast. Von Kleist had given the order to Guderian to cross the Meuse at 1500 on 13 May. Guderian asked for more time as 2 Panzer Division was lagging behind and his engineers were hardly ready after all their efforts in the Ardennes. Von Kleist's air plan for 13 May was the opposite of the plans Guderian had made with General Loerzer; instead of continuous support to keep the gunners' heads down, von Kleist had ordered a mass attack, coinciding with the start of the artillery bombardment. Nevertheless, the order stood and Guderian flew back to his command post. He now had a very short time to issue his own orders, so taking those for the war games out of the files, all that had to be done was to change the time of the attack from 0900 to 1500 hours.

13 May: Over the Meuse

Rommel started the day very early. By 0300 he was in Dinant, having left his command vehicle, and made his way on foot to the bank of the Meuse. Here the 6th Rifle Regiment was attempting to cross in rubber boats, but was being held by converging fire from the west bank. As the mist began to clear, not having a smoke-screen unit, Rommel ordered a number of houses to be set alight. He had in the meantime ordered 7th Motor Cycle Battalion to clear the west bank of the river, but when he visited their position by tank he found that the crossing was now stopped altogether, though a company had succeeded in getting across the river. On his return to Divisional Headquarters to confer briefly with the Army Commander and General Hoth, the Corps Commander, Rommel arranged for some Panzers III and IV and a troop of artillery to be put at his disposal. Returning to Leffé he eventually reached the weir and the crossing-point nearby where his men were pinned to the ground. Soon the extra tanks arrived and, supported by the artillery, drove slowly north 'at 50 yards' spacing' along the valley. Covered by this fire the crossing slowly got underway again. Rommel crossed in one of the first boats and for a while took command of the troops on the far side. Here two companies were making good progress when suddenly enemy tanks were reported. Rommel immediately ordered every weapon to open fire and drove the tanks back. It was a surprise attack indeed, as the companies had no anti-tank guns at that stage. Returning to the east bank, Rommel

then drove up to the 6th Rifle Regiment crossing-point. Here he learned that the commander of the anti-tank battalion had got twenty guns over the river and that engineers were starting to build an 8-ton pontoon bridge. Ordering them to build a 16-ton pontoon bridge instead, he crossed with his signals vehicle to visit the Brigade Headquarters that had been set up on the west bank. In Granges the situation was critical as the French had launched a heavy attack with tanks. The commander of the 7th Motor Cycle Battalion had been wounded and his adjutant killed. Returning to cross the river, Rommel ordered the panzer regiment to cross that night. But to get tanks over the 120-yard wide river by night was to prove a very slow task – by dawn only fifteen tanks had been transported across the river.

It is clear from this account that both the Belgian Chasseurs Ardennais as well as the French

German troops crossing the Meuse in a 4-man rubber dinghy.

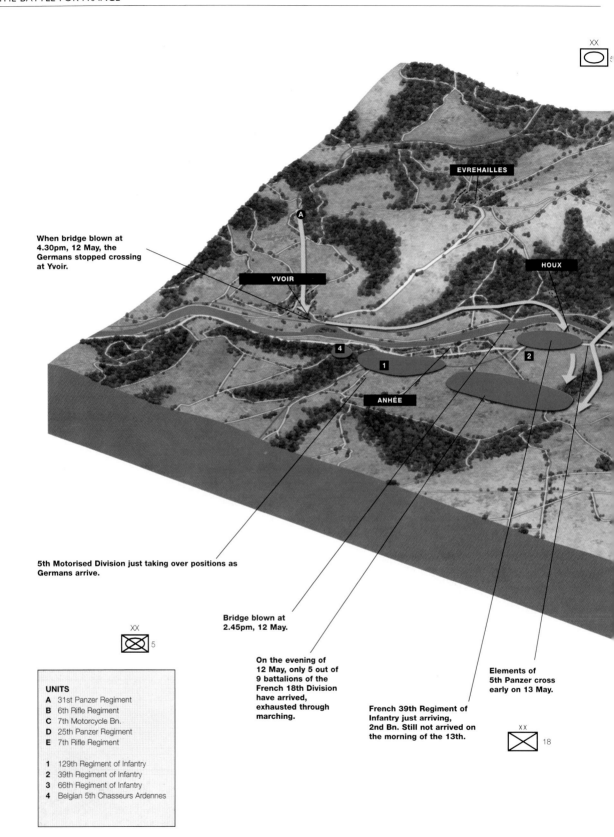

When bridge blown at 4.30pm, 12 May, the Germans stopped crossing at Yvoir.

EVREHAILLES

HOUX

YVOIR

ANHÉE

5th Motorised Division just taking over positions as Germans arrive.

Bridge blown at 2.45pm, 12 May.

On the evening of 12 May, only 5 out of 9 battalions of the French 18th Division have arrived, exhausted through marching.

Elements of 5th Panzer cross early on 13 May.

French 39th Regiment of Infantry just arriving, 2nd Bn. Still not arrived on the morning of the 13th.

UNITS

A   31st Panzer Regiment
B   6th Rifle Regiment
C   7th Motorcycle Bn.
D   25th Panzer Regiment
E   7th Rifle Regiment

1   129th Regiment of Infantry
2   39th Regiment of Infantry
3   66th Regiment of Infantry
4   Belgian 5th Chasseurs Ardennes

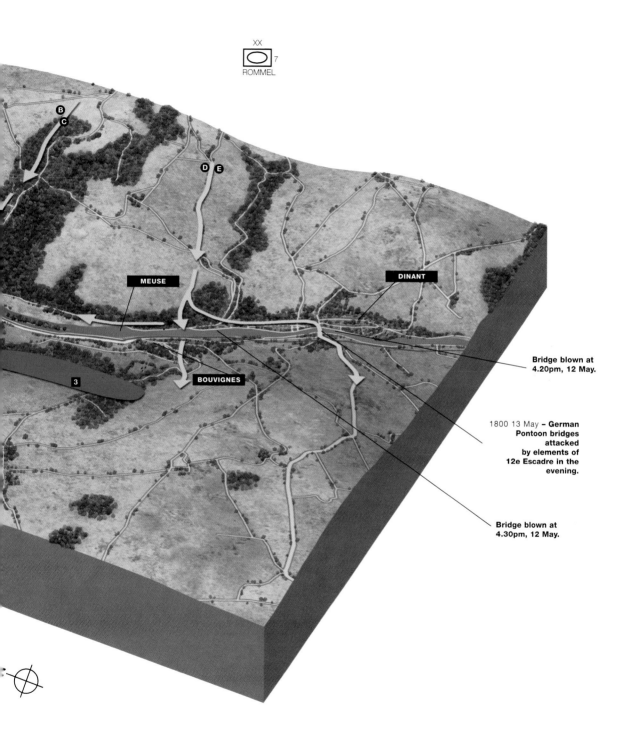

XX
7
ROMMEL

B
C

D E

MEUSE

DINANT

3

BOUVIGNES

Bridge blown at
4.20pm, 12 May.

1800 13 May – German
Pontoon bridges
attacked
by elements of
12e Escadre in the
evening.

Bridge blown at
4.30pm, 12 May.

MEUSE CROSSINGS AT DINANT AND HOUX, 12-13 MAY 1940

66th Regiment fought hard to man the pillboxes and bunkers on the Meuse. By dark there were still pockets behind the German bridgehead, but a relieving force was needed very urgently. To the rear there was confusion and delay. General Boucher found, some five hours after he first learnt of the crossing at Houx, that he had lost all contact with the battalion of the 39th Regiment. To try and find them he pushed forward motor-cycle troops and machine-gun carriers, which were thrown back. He then decided to launch a battalion of the 129th Regiment on Haut-le-Wastia. The time of the attack was to be 1300 hours, but nothing happened until 1400 hours, when the attack was immediately dispersed by aircraft. Then he ordered a regiment of Motorized Dragoons from II Corps to take over the attack, but they could not start until 2000 hours, so the operation was postponed until the following morning.

Meanwhile 18 Division HQ was also in trouble, as communications became almost non-existent during the day. As General Doumene remarked: 'Lines were cut. They had ceased with the 77th and could not be re-established with the 128th. The radio did not function. There were no more motor cycles.' During the afternoon General Martin had ordered the colonel of the 39th to counter-attack Surinvaux and clear the enemy off the west bank of the Meuse. The operation would be supported by three artillery groups and a squadron of tanks. The attack was due to open at 1930 hours. Two postponements then took place as the regiment was not ready. Finally the tanks went forward at 2000 hours but, without the infantry to consolidate, finally withdrew with a handful of prisoners. Little if any of all this filtered back to the French High Command. Then in the late afternoon news reached them from Huntziger, and later that night General Georges rang Gamelin saying that 'a rather serious pin-prick had taken place at Sedan'!

Guderian's orders for the crossings at Sedan were simple. If 2 Panzer arrived in time it would cross at Donchery, while 1 Panzer would cross at

A French Hotchkiss tank halted under cover.

Glaire, and at Torcy in the northern part of Sedan; 10 Panzer Division would cross south of Sedan and protect the left flank. The main thrust was to be by Kirchner's Panzer Division, which would be reinforced by the Grossdeutschland Regiment, an entire battalion of assault engineers, and the heavy artillery battalions belonging to the other two divisions. Behind Guderian's group of panzers, von Wietersheim's XIV Motorized Corps was assembling to support and exploit his success.

As the morning passed, more and more German tanks and artillery poured forward and occupied every nook and cranny of the ground near the crossing-points. On the French side the high Bois de la Marfée feature looked down on it all, and the French artillery made the most of such an excellent observation point. But strangely the amount of ammunition had been limited to between thirty and eighty rounds per gun; for, as General Lafontaine said, 'the enemy would be unable to do anything for four to six days, as it would take them this long to bring up heavy artillery and ammunition and to position them'.

But had the French taken the Luftwaffe into account? The two commanders Loerzer and von Richthofen controlled nearly 1,500 aircraft, which stood ready to attack on just a few miles of front. This opened at 0700 hours when the Dornier Do 17 bombers started softening up the communications of the artillery and also the headquarters. As the bombing grew in intensity, with repeated breaks in the telephone lines, the French artillery fire grew less, while the commanders on the ground began to complain that their positions were being bombed without any intervention by Allied fighters. It seems extraordinary that so little was attempted to prevent this, but much blame must go to the French High Command, because when d'Astier was asked to give priority for air support to Second Army he was given no hint of a German river-crossing, Billotte only referring to 'the next two or three days'. As for the RAF under Barratt, their losses over the past

Large French artillery piece firing from a camouflaged position.

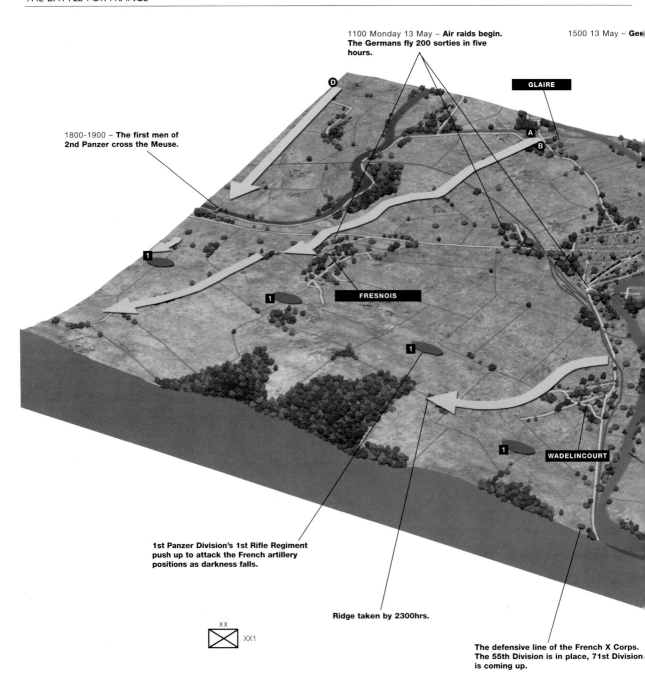

1100 Monday 13 May – Air raids begin. The Germans fly 200 sorties in five hours.

1500 13 May – Ger

GLAIRE

D

A

B

1800-1900 – The first men of 2nd Panzer cross the Meuse.

FRESNOIS

WADELINCOURT

1st Panzer Division's 1st Rifle Regiment push up to attack the French artillery positions as darkness falls.

Ridge taken by 2300hrs.

The defensive line of the French X Corps. The 55th Division is in place, 71st Division is coming up.

XX1

UNITS
A 1st Panzer Division
B SS Regiment Grossdeutschland
C 10th Panzer Division
D 2nd Panzer Division

1 French Artillery positions

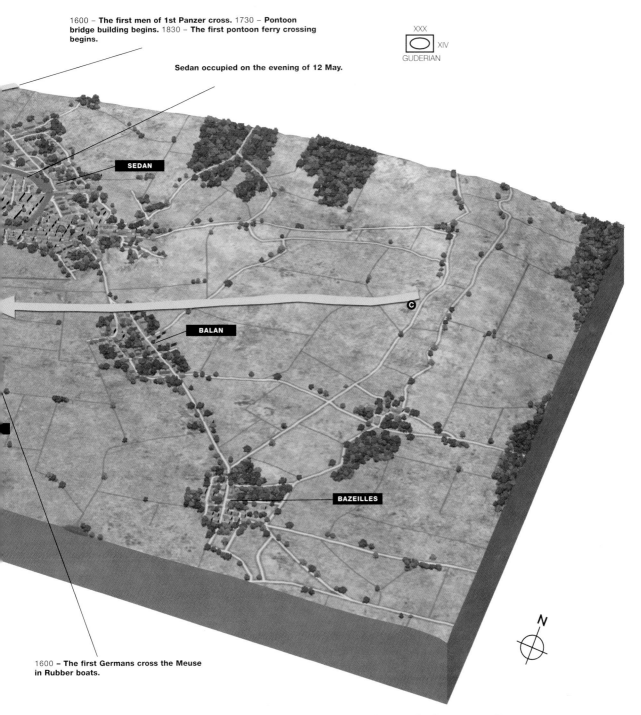

fires on French positions.

1600 – **The first men of 1st Panzer cross.** 1730 – **Pontoon bridge building begins.** 1830 – **The first pontoon ferry crossing begins.**

Sedan occupied on the evening of 12 May.

XXX
XIV
GUDERIAN

SEDAN

BALAN

BAZEILLES

N

1600 – **The first Germans cross the Meuse in Rubber boats.**

MEUSE CROSSINGS AT SEDAN, 13-14 MAY 1940

three days had been very heavy, and on 13 May there were only 72 out of 135 serviceable bombers available. The French fighters flew 250 sorties on the Ninth and Second Army fronts, shooting down 21 and losing twelve aircraft – figures hardly worth mentioning compared with flights of 50 German bombers protected by 80 Messerschmitts attacking beyond Sedan.

About noon the Stukas began to come in '... hundreds of planes in dense formations ... the Stukas operated in three groups, each of about forty planes; the first, coming in at about 5,000 feet,

Aerial photograph of the centre of Sedan, showing two bridges across the River Meuse destroyed.

'Bombs away!' – a Stuka, having released its bombs, begins to pull out from its dive.

German training exercise designed to practise troops in crossing the River Meuse in rubber boats.

would attack with two or three planes at a time while the second group hovered watchfully at 12,000 feet, looking for the targets missed by the first group and then – after they had expended their bombs – moving in in turn; the third group operated in isolation, picking out single or moving targets. After the Stuka waves, the Dorniers would resume their work; then more Stukas. Around them buzzed the Me 109s and the heavier Me 110 "destroyers", pouncing on any slower French fighter that attempted to get at the vulnerable Stukas.' Alistair Horne writes, 'The explosive force of the heavy bombs literally turned batteries upside down, wrecked guns and filled the working parts of anti-aircraft machine-guns with earth and grit. Observers in concrete bunkers were blinded by the dust and smoke and everywhere telephone lines were ruptured. The noise was terrifying.'

At 14.30 hours Guderian's artillery opened up with its barrage, while the flak gunners, taking advantage of the Stukas' bombing, switched to the river's edge to engage the bunkers on the opposite bank. At close range these 20mm (twin barrelled) and 37mm automatic cannon were very effective where the embrasures had not been finished, and the Krupp 88mm anti-aircraft gun could more than compete by direct fire with the reinforced bunkers designed to hold off the oblique fire of guns up to 210mm.

On the left of the German attack, 10 Panzer Division was unlucky in that guns to the south opposite Bazeilles had not been touched by the Stukas' attack. These guns were able to fire on the Division's left-hand regiment, the 69th, as it attempted to cross. Of fifty small rubber dinghies, all but two were destroyed in the first rush. It was the men of the assault engineers who initially succeeded, as an account by Feldwebel Rubarth records. Rubarth had a group of eleven engineers. Putting four into each of two rubber dinghies, each intended to carry three men, he crossed the river under intense fire. During the crossing he ordered his driver, Corporal Podszus, to engage the slits of the nearest bunker with a machine-gun, using another man's shoulder to steady the aim. As soon as the dingy reached the bank, Rubarth succeeded in silencing this bunker and led his men into dead ground to the rear of the next bunker. This time he used an explosive charge which ripped out the rear wall. Soon the French defenders surrendered. 'Thus encouraged we flung ourselves at two further fieldworks we had spotted some 100 metres half-left of us.' The first was attacked by Corporal Bräutigam; Rubarth with his sergeant and two of the corporals took the second one, and the first line of bunkers had been broken.

Rubarth then reached the railway embankment about a hundred yards from the river. Here he came again under heavy fire and with his ammunition exhausted decided to get back for reinforcements and ammunition, but the crossings had again been halted by heavy fire. The French meanwhile launched an attack, and Bräutigam was killed and two corporals wounded before Rubarth's little party could beat them back. Soon, however, some of the riflemen and some engineers succeeded in getting over the river and Rubarth advanced again to open a gap in the second line of bunkers. By nightfall, with the riflemen of 86th Regiment, Rubarth finally reached his objective on the high ground above Wadelincourt. Of his group of eleven, he lost that day six dead and three wounded. He was immediately awarded the Ritterkreuz and a lieutenant's commission.

On 1 Panzer Division's sector at Sedan, the task of crossing the Meuse was allotted to the Regiment Grossdeutschland. This was an élite force that always fought as a separate unit and had been earmarked by Guderian since February to smash a hole in the French lines. Accustomed to ceremonial duties, the Regiment had drawn from Guderian a remark about infantry who 'slept

A German major steering a wooden assault boat. These keelless boats took 16 men and were powered by 12hp engines.

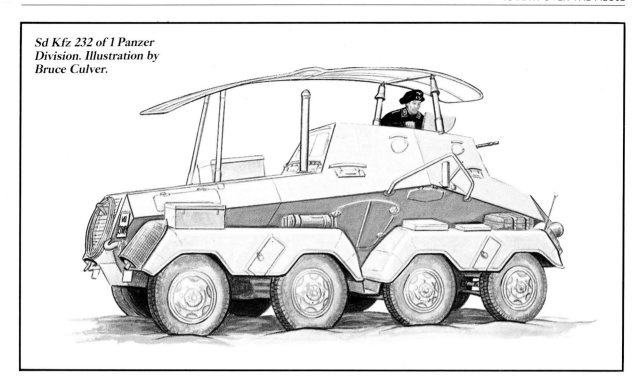

Sd Kfz 232 of 1 Panzer Division. Illustration by Bruce Culver.

instead of advancing at night'. At this, its colonel, Lieutenant-Colonel Graf von Schwerin, had bet Guderian a case of champagne that this would not happen to his regiment. So throughout April it had carried out tough exercises including, of course, river-crossings and night attacks.

Shortly before the time of the attack the leading companies chosen for the actual crossing set off from Floing less than a mile from the River Meuse. The crossing-point was near a cloth factory overlooking the river, and all the way down the French guns were silent. Then, as the Germans broke cover and dashed forward with the assault boats, the fire came down and the engineers could not reach the river. Assault guns were called up but failed to silence the fire from the line of bunkers on the far bank; then an 88mm flak gun tried, but this, too, failed to silence the fire that swept across the river. More boats were brought up but could not be launched. Then a second 88mm was brought in against the bunkers, and finally part of the leading company succeeded in crossing – quickly to be followed by a second company of the Grossdeutschlanders. The two companies fought their way forward towards the main road from Sedan to Donchery. Here more bunkers were taken, and at about 1700 hours men from

Lieutenant-Colonel Balck's 1st Rifle Regiment, the motorized infantry of 1 Panzer, joined the attack to reach their objective, the high ground. The fighting at several points was very fierce, but finally, in failing light, the objective was taken. Now 1 Panzer Division had a good bridgehead with six of its battalions well established, and a large part of the important la Marfée heights was in their hands. Meanwhile the division's motorcycle battalion had crossed over the Meuse loop at Iges and had cleared the whole peninsula before joining Balck.

Guderian had no tanks over the Meuse, and priority had to be given to this urgent task. By mid-afternoon the engineers had arrived. As they started unloading, an enemy bombing attack came in. Their nine machine-guns were ready, however, and the bombs fell far off. Then French artillery fire started, but the spotter aircraft was driven off by German fighters and the fire came down some fifty yards away from the spot where the engineers were erecting the bridge. At about midnight the sixteen-ton bridge was ready and the tanks started to cross.

Unexpectedly, on the morning of 13 May, 2 Panzer made much better progress and by the middle of the afternoon had begun to reach Donchery. This was where the crossing had been planned, but when the tanks reached the banks of

*French tanks waiting
under cover.*

the Meuse they were met by intense artillery fire. Although pinned down, the tanks helped the assault engineers to launch a boat; first one and then another was shot away and the attempts were temporarily abandoned. The exchange of fire continued for some time until one of the bunkers was silenced and the engineers succeeded in

crossing – making a hole which was gradually widened.

Despite the valour of some of the French, many of the permanent defences were unfinished and once the Germans broke the chain their reinforcement continued throughout the night. Guderian's orders for 2 Panzer were precise and ambitious; having seized the high ground behind Donchery it was then to swing immediately

westward, cross the Ardennes Canal and then roll up the enemy defences along the Meuse. It looked a pretty tough proposition. Sinister events, however, were about to intervene in favour of the Germans.

General Lafontaine's 55 Division occupied an ideal natural position at la Marfée, and had very strong artillery support. Some of its men had shown unsung heroism and many of the bunkers had been defended desperately. In the open, however,

matters had been different and they seem to have melted away. News of the crossings had been fragmentary and it was only late on 13 May that Huntziger heard anything that caused him concern. At about 1830, however, Gransard received a report from a battery commander at Chaumont that tanks had been seen at la Marfée. Shortly after this the colonel commanding the corps heavy artillery at Bulson had phoned his commander (Poncelet) saying that heavy fighting had broken out some 400 yards from his command post, and that they were German machine-guns and he would be encircled within five minutes; could he withdraw? He was given the order to do so by Poncelet, who now evacuated his own post behind Bulson and gave orders for the withdrawal of his own batteries. No German tanks had crossed yet and certainly no German infantrymen were anywhere near Bulson. Colonel Poncelet, ordered back later that night, committed suicide some twelve days later but the damage had been done.

General Lafontaine's command post was just behind Bulson, and about three hours after the first crossing had taken place he had just sent a battalion to reinforce la Marfée when suddenly a crowd of terrified men came down the road. 'The tanks are at Bulson,' they shouted. Officers were there and gunners and men of 55 Division, firing their rifles indiscriminately, all mixed together. Many claimed to have seen the tanks at Bulson and Chaumont; worse still, commanders actually pretended to have received orders to withdraw. General Lafontaine and his officers had tried to halt this rabble and to reason with them, all to no avail. Lafontaine now requested Grandsard to be allowed to move his command post back to Chémery. But here he found matters far worse, as '... the flood of fugitives traverses the village without pause; all the echelons of the division, accumulated in this region – fighting units, regimental HQs, supply columns, vehicle parks ... all are heading for the south, swelled by stragglers; as if by magic, their officers have naturally received a mysterious order to withdraw'.

Meanwhile Grandsard had relayed to General Baudet the news of the tanks at Chaumont and Bulson. Baudet had then moved his newly established command post at Raucourt back three or four miles and took with him the commander of the divisional artillery. The absence of authority, however, quickly led to a number of the guns being abandoned or even destroyed out of hand. One report gave '... three out of four groups of 75s having been abandoned and four out of six of the heavy artillery'. Too few of the battery commanders had followed the example of Major Beneditti of the 363rd Regiment, who manhandled his guns forward during the night – against the flood of men who claimed they had received orders to withdraw.

14 May

General Grandsard had the 4th and 7th Tank Battalions and the 205th and 213th Infantry Regiments in reserve, and these were now put at Lafontaine's disposal. Meanwhile 3 Armoured Division and 3 Motorized Division were now arriving and were at Huntziger's disposal. On the morning of 14 May at 0130, Lafontaine ordered the four reserve regiments to carry out a two-pronged attack commencing at 0400 hours. This could have caught the Germans without the tank support they

so badly needed, but it never got off the ground. Lieutenant-Colonel Labarthe succeeded in persuading Lafontaine that he could not risk taking the 213th Regiment up against the tide of refugees pouring back, while the 7th Tank Battalion said that they never received the orders. The 205th Regiment got held up by lorries packed with men who shouted, 'The Boches are there – don't go forward,' and was then halted by a dispatch rider. Finally the 4th Tank Battalion, told by a staff officer that the panzers were at Chaumont, decided to halt for the night. Consequently the counter-attack did not start until 0700 hours, by which time the whole German situation had changed.

In the centre, Lieutenant-Colonel Balck had rallied his weary battalion and led them on a five-mile march towards the south. By dawn they had reached Chéhéry; while on the left flank, as the fire from 71 Division had fallen off, the crossing now started in earnest, and engineers started a bridge for 10 Panzer Division. As the panzers moved

A French heavy gun in a hastily dug-in position.

across, the bridgehead was about three miles wide and up to six miles deep.

On 13 May, Reinhardt's XLI Corps was halted at Monthermé, and indeed was held up for two days. Unlike Guderian's sector at Sedan, there was little Luftwaffe support allocated to Reinhardt, and the French troops were regulars of 102 Fortress Division who had been dug-in ever since the start of the war. But Corap had taken the view that the Charleville–Mézières Gap was the most vulnerable part of the sector and had put most of his artillery there, leaving the 42nd half-brigade of colonial machine-gunners to defend Monthermé. Here the high ground dropped down several hundreds of feet to the Meuse which flowed round the Monthermé isthmus with the half-submerged girders of the destroyed road bridge. It was a poor crossing point compared with some of the others. Now the Mark III and IV panzers were ordered forward to fire at the well-concealed French bunkers, but as the men of the 4th Rifle Regiment ran forward to their dinghies they were met by a devastating fire and were unable to launch the boats. Eventually a carefully camouflaged bunker beneath a café was spotted by the tanks and destroyed. Then it was found, quite by chance, that some dinghies launched upstream had drifted against the spans of the broken bridge, where they seemed to be out of the line of fire. Rapidly the engineers exploited their opportunity and erected a footbridge by lashing planks together. Then the rest of the battalion got across in the darkening light. Once over they dug in. Nevertheless, the chances of getting any tanks over the next day seemed slim.

In Holland the events of 13 May had brought the Dutch to the point of exhaustion, with 9 Panzer Division on the outskirts of Rotterdam. Elsewhere Giraud's Seventh Army was back near the estuary of the Scheldt, while the Belgians were behind the Dyle line, alongside the BEF. So it was Prioux's Cavalry Corps that stood in front and did the fighting with the tanks of 3 and 4 Panzer Divisions attacking the two light mechanized divisions throughout the day. The fiercest fighting took place around Merdorp, and there were heavy losses on both sides. The French fought with great tenacity, but too often they were in small numbers and often

German infantryman. Illustration by Richard Geiger.

outmanoeuvred, while the Germans found it difficult to compete with the French Somuas. During the night Prioux drew his tanks back behind the Belgian anti-tank obstacle at Perez.

That night General Georges called a meeting with General Doumene on 14 May. Georges was terribly pale. He announced, 'Our front has been pushed in at Sedan! There have been some failures ...' Falling into a chair he was silenced by a sob. Gamelin, however, remained quite ignorant of Georges' state of mind. Indeed, had not Georges reported that the Second Army was 'holding' and had added, 'Here we are calm ...'?

In Rommel's sector, an attack by the French 14th Motorized Dragoons had captured the village of Haut-le-Wastia and taken some motorcyclists, but had then withdrawn. Meanwhile the 7th Rifle Regiment had advanced overnight as far as Onhaye. Here it was heavily engaged. Then Rommel received a message from Bismarck, commander of the 7th Rifles, that he was 'encircled'; in fact, it was mistakenly encoded for 'arrived', but Rommel did not know this and hurried forward with the handful of tanks that had got over the Meuse. Onhaye was the key to high ground leading directly on to open country westwards towards Philippeville and the plains of northern France. Rommel, now in a Mark III tank, followed closely behind the fighting until the tank

A Hurricane fighter squadron on patrol in France.

A French anti-tank gun with team.

was hit and plunged down a slope, where it was in full view of the French defence. Screened by smoke from burning smoke-candles on another tank, Rommel managed to extricate himself, but it had been a lucky escape. The capture of the high ground was only achieved late in the day. How different it might have been if the French 1 Armoured Division had been able to attack Rommel on 13 May, or even 14 May at Onhaye! Fifty per cent of this division's 150 tanks were 'B' models, but on the other hand it had no armoured cars or signals units. The division had been under pressure to reach Charleroi where it remained inactive on 13 May, because Billotte was worried about the Gembloux Gap. Then at midnight on 13/14 May it was ordered to Florennes, but owing to the congestion on the roads it took seven hours to cover the twenty miles. It was short of petrol and it

was only at midnight that all three battalions were assembled. Meanwhile the petrol carriers had been sent to the rear and it was doubtful if the division **would be able to attack early on 15 May.**

On the Onhaye front, 4 North African Division was fighting well, but on its left, by the Houx crossing, the battalion of 39th Regiment had been rounded up by the Germans advancing with tanks at daybreak. With the Luftwaffe attacking, the remains of 66th Regiment were overcome. The line was broken irredeemably and ebbed back towards the Anthée–Sosoye defence lines.

But worse was to come. North of Dinant, at Yvoir, a German infantry division had crossed, while another infantry division was crossing at Givet. Here, in the absence of his commander, the French Chief of Staff ordered 22 Division to fall back some six miles. General Corap was furious

and ordered an immediate counter-attack. But it was too late; the division's morale had given way and it was soon to disintegrate.

Meanwhile Rommel's tanks were advancing beyond Onhaye and by nightfall had reached Anthée; behind, more and more panzers were crossing the pontoon bridge. The French ahead were still fighting hard, but General Martin, worried about both 18 and 22 Divisions, gave orders for the whole corps to fall back behind a line through Florennes.

Further south, at Monthermé, the colonial machine-gunners of 102 Fortress Division were repeatedly counter-attacking the German riflemen who had succeeded in crossing. The footbridge over the river had been destroyed by artillery fire and Kempff told Reinhardt that he could see little chance of making progress and that there was no question of building a bridge to get tanks over.

Halfway between Monthermé and Charleville was the town of Nouzonville. Here two of the infantry divisions from General Hasse's III Corps got down to the river where they were confronted by devastating fire from 102 Fortress Division. At

their third attempt at a crossing, however, they managed to get a foothold on the far bank.

Now we must return to Sedan, as it is there that the change in direction of Guderian's attack took place. A number of the tanks of 1 Panzer Division had already got across the bridge by dawn, with many more queuing up, and headed towards Chéhéry and Bulson. This was also the objective of the two counter-attacking groups. As the right-hand group of the French 4th Tank Battalion and 205th Infantry Regiment were still not ready, only 7th Tank Battalion and Labathe's 213rd Infantry Regiment were advancing, somewhat piecemeal, against the German armour. The infantry had no anti-tank guns at all and the artillery support was doubtful, while 7th Tank Battalion was armed with the 37mm gun on the light FCM tank. Approaching Chéhéry at about 0800 hours, a sharp encounter broke out when 7th Tank Battalion surprised some tanks of 1 Panzer refuelling. Two German tanks were knocked out and Colonel Keltsch was badly wounded.

Shortly afterwards General Georges was reporting to Gamelin that '... the breach at Sedan

Sd Kfz 231 of 2 Panzer Division. Illustration by Bruce Culver.

Cross-country training: German infantry in the attack.

has been contained and a counter-attack with strong formations was carried out at 4.30 am'. But now the circumstances had changed, for German Sturmpioniers hurled hollow charges under the tracks of the French tanks, killing their commander. While a number of anti-tank guns and two 88mm came into action, more tanks of 1 Panzer were assembling to outflank the French, and accounted for eleven out of fifteen tanks near the little village of Connage. German tanks now broke through the unprotected flank of the 213th Regiment which lost heavily and was soon in retreat. French tanks on the high ground near Bulson were unable to hold fast, and 7th Tank Battalion was forced back with the loss of more than half their machines. Lafontaine did not hear of the failure of this attack until 2130 hours and ordered the right-hand group to withdraw behind Raucourt. Now 55 Division no longer existed, and two days later Lafontaine would be removed from command.

The same fate now befell 71 Division. Here General Baudet had moved his command post twice in fourteen hours and had lost all contact with his troops. Except for 205th Regiment which continued to hold out around Raucourt, 71 Division had begun to break up. Cries of 'Tanks to the rear and to the left!' had been passed from group to group and, sweeping up the artillerymen, they had joined the flood of men in full retreat. During the morning Grandsard put through a call to Huntziger but found the exchange did not reply. His chief Signals Officer had completely evacuated the exchange without orders. Of his artillery he had only two heavy guns and his only intact division, 3 North African, had been transferred to XVIII Corps. What was left of Grandsard's command was transferred to General Flavigny, and the newly constituted XXI Corps, containing 3 Armoured Division and 3 Motorized Division, was ordered up towards Sedan.

Throughout the morning of 14 May Guderian had been able to judge what was happening on his front. Then the failure of Lafontaine's counter-attack and the lack of any immediate follow-up showed the weakness of the French position. Motoring to 1 Panzer, which was then on the line

Chémery–Maisoncelle, he asked Kirchner if he could turn his division westward, or whether a flank guard should be left facing south on the Ardennes Canal? Major Wenck replied *'Klotzen, nicht kleckern'* – literally, 'Wallop them, don't tap them.' Guderian immediately gave orders for both 1 and 2 Panzer Divisions to change direction west and to break clean through the French defences. He was taking a grave risk in turning away from the French reinforcements that German intelligence was warning were on the way. But Stonne was the key to this southern flank, and here he would leave 10 Panzer Division and the Grossdeutschland Regiment. To Kirchner, Guderian gave the dramatic instruction 'To the right, wheel, road map Rethel!'

The French forces holding the River Bar on the front that Guderian was now taking consisted of 5 DLC and 1 Cavalry Brigade. Both had suffered quite severely in the Ardennes. With them was 3 Spahi Brigade and, ostensibly, 53 Division (a 'B' class formation). This latter had been marched and counter-marched over two days and it would not reach the Bar to be of use on 14 May. The French cavalry had fought hard and put up a fine resistance, but by nightfall on the 14th Balck's riflemen had reached their objective at Singly. 1 Panzer's tanks had also been in action and its losses had mounted until only three-quarters of its tanks were fit for action. But the German gains had been considerable – some 3,000 prisoners, fifty tanks and twenty-eight guns.

Meanwhile the French 3 Armoured Division and the Motorized Infantry Division were painfully moving up towards Sedan. The former was a brand-new division with two battalions of Hotchkiss H-39 light tanks. With excellent morale it had, however, only started training on 1 May. It had suffered considerable delay during its move to the front from damage to the roads and bridges, and had no engineers to carry out repairs. Also the heavy 'B' tanks had difficulty in crossing the Aisne. Getting nearer the front the tanks had been met by the horde of fugitives who had blocked the roads with vehicles of every kind during their precipitate retreat. The armoured division eventually reached its assembly area behind Stonne at 0600 hours on 14 May. Here it received conflicting orders – to contain the pocket of enemy, and to counter-attack at the earliest possible moment. The commander of 3 Armoured pointed out to Flavigny that the division had only just completed a thirty-mile night march and would not be ready to attack for some ten hours. He suggested 1600 hours for the time of the attack, but Flavigny ordered 1100 hours. This became 1300 hours owing to refuelling, and then as a result of the bombing, and waves of refugees, it was 1600 hours before the division was ready. Meanwhile 3 Motorized Division had been delayed in its approach march even more than 3 Armoured, and only produced three reconnaissance groups.

Huntziger had moved his HQ to Verdun, and Flavigny was alone at Senuc. Now he made a fateful decision – he would abandon the attack, but contain the enemy. This was decided at 1530 hours, and 3 Armoured Division then had to spread out some twelve miles from Omont west of the Bar to Stonne, one 'B' and two H-39 tanks in a series of stops. At 1900 hours Huntziger's Chief of Staff told Georges that the attack had been held up for technical reasons, and Huntziger himself spoke shortly afterwards saying that the enemy advance had been '… contained by Flavigny's *groupement* between the Ardennes Canal and the Meuse'. Georges replied sharply that the attack must go in the next day.

By now, Huntziger was getting very depressed and made a grave error in considering that Guderian's thrust was aimed at outflanking the Maginot Line and rolling it up from the north. He planned to counter this by swinging back the centre of his army to a position further back at Inor; in other words, he was pulling away from Ninth Army and widening the very gap through which Guderian was about to advance.

Late on the night of 14 May, General Corap also took a decision that opened up the gap even more. Telephoning Billotte, he told him that he intended pulling back to the frontier positions he had left earlier. Billotte agreed in principle but told him to establish 'an intermediate stop line' roughly along the road from Charleroi to Rethel. But this order produced more confusion, some units making for the position behind Florennes ordered by General Martin, some making for the intermediate line; others did not get the order at all and simply struggled westwards on their own.

A French 2.5cm
Hotchkiss anti-tank gun.

On 14 May ten British Battles had bombed the pontoons at Sedan without loss. This early morning raid, however, had caused minimal damage, which was speedily repaired. Then in mid-morning the French bombers attacked in two raids; against troop concentrations on the west bank of the Meuse and on the outskirts of Sedan. Six of the bombers were brought down and the damage they inflicted was again negligible. In the afternoon, however, Barratt threw in every available Blenheim and Battle, seventy-one in all. Forty did not return – the greatest loss to be suffered by the RAF in this campaign. No less than 250 Allied fighters had taken part as escorts, but the Luftwaffe mustered 814 aircraft that day. However, it was the flak concentrated with determination around the pontoon bridges that really brought the considerable losses to the bombers who were desperately trying to hit the narrow target. The bridges were not destroyed. Although the supplies being taken over the Meuse were delayed, they were never halted.

That morning, negotiations began between the German and Dutch representatives for a cease-fire, but at 1400 hours sixty He 111s bombed the old city of Rotterdam for twenty minutes and killed nearly 900 people in a brutal raid. Holland signed her capitulation that night. Further south the BEF were engaged when Montgomery's artillery foiled attempts by General von Bock's infantry to take Louvain. Prioux's tanks meanwhile had repulsed a determined effort by Hoepner's panzers to break through the Belgian anti-tank obstacle, but its losses had been considerable. Now the cavalry had been pulled back behind General Blanchard's main line.

15 May: German Exploitation

On 15 May Rommel gave orders for 7 Panzer Division to 'thrust straight through in one stride' to the Cerfontaine area, which was eight miles to the west of Philippeville. Rommel rode with the tanks leading this advance. At about 0800 hours he learnt that the Luftwaffe would give him Stuka support and he called them to operate immediately in front of his own tanks. Then suddenly the column burst upon the tanks of the French Armoured Division which had been awaiting fuel lorries. Two battalions of 'B' tanks were caught at close range

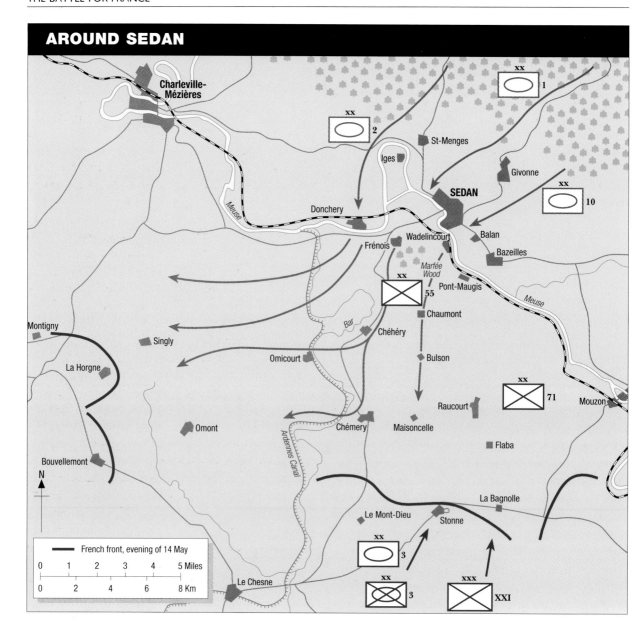

AROUND SEDAN

and a sharp battle began. One company of French tanks counter-attacked and their superior fire did some damage to the Germans. But then Rommel pulled away, leaving 5 Panzer to finish the job.

The French commander, Bruneau, ordered the tanks to regroup north of Florennes, but it was too late as at that moment Verner's 5 Panzer Division was on them. By the late afternoon the French 1 Armoured Division had been reduced to six of its 'B' tanks. While only one of its light battalions had taken part in the action, this too had suffered severely. The French had fought hard and claimed

to have knocked out a hundred of the German tanks – a figure which may have been exaggerated. But when Bruneau saw the division behind the frontier positions next day, it only had seventeen tanks left; the remainder had for one reason or another not managed to withdraw after the action.

Meanwhile Rommel was out in the open, making for Philippeville and pushing on to Cerfontaine eight miles beyond. Everything was done at speed; when the tanks were fired upon they replied without stopping and this immediate action seemed to be the answer to all attempts to halt the column. Prisoners were collected as they drove furiously along, or just disarmed and told to march back to the German rear. The men of both panzer divisions were getting very tired and many of their vehicles were in need of attention, but Rommel throughout the whole day drove them on. At Cerfontaine, where the laager formed that night, Rommel could feel very proud of his achievements. His losses had amounted to fifteen killed and he had knocked out or captured 75 tanks and taken many prisoners. But far more to his credit was the fact that he was through the stop line before it had even been partially manned. His advance was a decisive blow to the French Ninth Army.

Pursued by the Luftwaffe, the remnants of the regiments in Ninth Army, who had started their withdrawal more or less in an orderly fashion, finished very broken up. Both 18 and 22 Divisions had all but disappeared; 4 North African Division had fought bravely at Anthée, but after losing its artillery which General Sancelme had sent back, it was cut up very badly near Philippeville.

At Monthermé very early on 15 May the German riflemen and engineers of 6 Panzer Division had attacked behind an artillery barrage. Using flame-throwers they had broken through the bunkers and by 0830 hours had captured the reserve positions. At this moment the bridging of the Meuse was completed for the tanks of 6 Panzer Division to cross. Further upstream the Infantry Division began erecting a bridge for 8 Panzer Division to cross. The race forward was now on. Having been driven from its positions and without any transport, the French 102 Fortress Division was quickly overpowered and the motorcycles of 6 Panzer raced onwards. Everywhere they passed scenes of devastation, abandoned guns, dead horses and men lying in the road and '... riderless horses roaming about, and often this scene escalated to regular barricades compounded of vehicles, guns and dead horses that had all been shot up together!' Von Stackelberg, a war diarist with one of the motorized infantry regiments, came on two German soldiers playing *We're going to hang out our washing on the Siegfried Line* on a 'liberated' gramophone. Standing nearby was a French Colonel who watched in dismay the columns of prisoners marching by. Every Frenchman von Stackelberg interrogated 'expressed hopeless amazement at the speed with which the Panzers had overrun them'.

On one road near Brunehamel four German tanks shot up a column of vehicles packed with French soldiers. In only a few hours these four tanks had captured five hundred prisoners and several hundred vehicles. 61 Division had seen little fighting; being a 'B' division, it had a certain amount of transport which it used in its withdrawal. Although some eight hundred of the division straggled back and others were picked up later, 61 Division was no longer a fighting force and by nightfall on 15 May Corap's Corps was no more. Still the panzers rushed on and by evening had captured Montcornet, thirty-seven miles from the Meuse. Then at midnight Reinhardt finally called a halt to this extraordinary march at Liart, seventeen miles beyond Montcornet.

At Sedan, Guderian had to break out westwards with 1 and 2 Panzer Divisions but he still had to protect his left flank in the vital sector of Stonne. Here was the threat of the counter-attack that had been postponed from the previous day. Chivied by both Georges and Huntziger, General Flavigny gave his orders at 1130 hours for 3 Armoured Division and 3 Motorized Division to attack at 1500 hours. The attack would be in line with French doctrine, in three bounds with infantry supported by tanks. The first line would be Chémery–Maisoncelle–Raucourt, the second the high ground south of Bulson and the third la Marfée–Pont-Maugis; the command would go to the infantryman, Bertin-Boussu of 3 Motorized Division. Then at 1430 Brocard reported that he could not collect his 'B' tanks in time. So the time of attack was put back to 1730 hours.

Meanwhile Grossdeutschland Regiment had advanced to the high ground on each side of Stonne, and throughout the 15th the battle swayed back and forth, the village changing hands several times. All available rifle companies from 10 Panzer Division were rushed forward to help stem the French attacks, and tanks were hurried up to meet an enemy tank thrust in the direction of Raucourt. Then at 1800 another strong attack came in on Chémery. This should have been the whole formal attack, but in fact it was made by only a battalion of

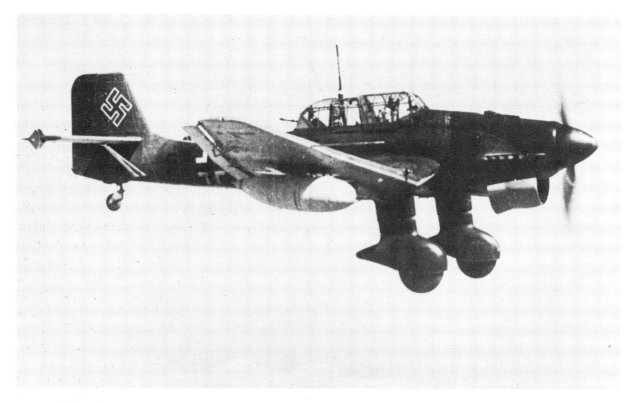

A Stuka dive-bomber...

... and the courage it took to face its attack.

'B' tanks and a handful of H-39s — and almost as soon as it had started it was called off by General Brocard!

The key to the defence of Stonne by the Germans was undoubtedly their skill and speed in deploying their anti-tank guns. During the action, which lasted more than ten hours, the German 14th Anti-tank Company lost a total of twenty-nine men, and six out of twelve guns with twelve vehicles were destroyed. But their skill and determination had knocked out thirty-three of the French tanks. The company commander, Lieutenant Beck-Broichsitter, and Oberfeldwebel Hindelang were both awarded the Ritterkreuz. That night both sides drew back from Stonne; but the Germans went back the next morning against only 'slight resistance'. Then the Grossdeutschland Regiment was pulled out and relieved by 29 Motorized Division, the first of XIV Corps to come up behind Guderian. Grossdeutschland had suffered heavy casualties, 103 killed and 459 wounded or missing – but the battle for Stonne had been won.

Guderian's 1 and 2 Panzer Divisions faced a new commander in their wheel right. General Touchon, whose 'Army Detachment Touchon, later became Sixth Army, had been given XLI Corps, 53 Division, a Cavalry groupement, 14 Division and, later on, 2 Armoured Division, together with the remains of Grandsard's X Corps. Commanded by General de Lattre de Tassigny, 14 Division was a fine regular division, sent from Lorraine, but only the 152nd Regiment arrived on time. This regiment and Marc's Spahi Brigade put up the main resistance to Guderian's attack. As before, the hardest fighting fell to Colonel Balck and his riflemen, and they were desperately tired. Balck's sheer determination carried them forward, however, until finally Bouvellemont was taken at nightfall. De Lattre's regiment, the 15th, had fought well and claimed some twenty tanks, but its casualties had been very heavy and all its anti-tank guns had been destroyed. At La Horgne, the 3 Spahis lost nineteen officers and a high proportion of other ranks and had resisted until 1800 hours when, with Colonel Marc captured and both regimental commanders killed, the brigade was overrun. It had fought with great courage but had not held back the men of 1 Panzer Division.

2 Panzer Division had an easier day. They had little difficulty in breaking through 53 Division and were soon making contact with Reinhardt's troops at Montcornet. Meanwhile the French 2 Armoured Division had been shuffled about and eventually arrived – or rather the tanks were to be unloaded from the railway at Hirson, but the road column was at Signy-l'Abbaye. While this was taking place, Reinhardt's panzers cut right through, destroying most of the artillery and driving the tanks to the north, while all the supply vehicles were across the Aisne on the south side. By dawn on 16 May the French armour was scattered over a huge area and the division had broken up without firing a shot.

On 15 May, General Georges had removed General Corap from his command and sent General Giraud in to fill the gap. On the evening of the following day Giraud sent Billotte a message expressing little hope. Then in the middle of the night he received the devastating news that the panzers were in Montcornet, twelve miles away! By midday General d'Astier had to admit that half of his fighter capacity had been knocked out and his bomber strength was down to 38. The RAF in France had a dozen Blenheims engaged against Rommel's columns near Dinant, but little else was possible, as the Battles were being withdrawn from daylight operations. So far, since the German attacks had started, twelve Hurricane squadrons had been sent to France and Reynaud asked Churchill to send another ten. This was urgently discussed by the British Cabinet. Air Chief Marshal Dowding objected vigorously, and finally his advice was accepted, but only after he had demonstrated that if more Hurricanes were sent to France, within a fortnight there would be none left in France or England. Meanwhile, a score of fighters were lost protecting the forward bases, and Air Marshal Barratt moved a number of his units south and his own Advanced HQ back to Coulommiers.

16 May

Guderian now was leaving the torn and battered fields around Sedan for open country that showed no signs of the destruction of war except where the roads were crowded with refugees fleeing before

A dejected group of Belgian refugees, who were streaming into France.

the panzers. Three panzer divisions were converging on Montcornet, and Guderian and Kempff of 6 Panzer Division fixed routes forward and then led the way. That evening, Guderian's leading units had reached Marle and Dercy on the River Serre, forty miles from their starting-point. Kempff captured Vervins and pushed forward as far as Guise on the Oise. Meanwhile 8 Panzer Division was pouring across a bridge built by 3 infantry Division at Nouzonville.

Further to the south, the French 2 Armoured Division was still struggling to get into some kind of shape, but found itself so scattered that its only contribution was a negative one in 'corking up' the crossing points over the Aisne. Some of the tanks cut off, or broken down, were engaged in isolated actions in which the crews fought bravely, but these inflicted only minor casualties, and underlined even more the mechanical weakness of the French 'B' tanks.

Rommel spent the morning of 16 May preparing to 'break through the Maginot Line' thinking the defences behind the French frontier to

be far more extensive than they really were. Opposite Rommel were the anti-tank obstacles and pillboxes manned by remnants of XI Corps, with a number of the pillboxes still locked up! As Rommel was about to issue orders the Army Commander, General von Kluge, arrived. He was more than satisfied with what he had seen and approved Rommel's plans. Rommel intended crossing the frontier near Sivry. The reconnaissance battalion would work on a wide front and the artillery would move up to Sivry. Then the panzer regiment under artillery cover would move up in extended order to the line of fortifications. Finally the rifle brigade under cover of tanks would take the fortifications and remove the barricades. Then the advance to Avesnes would start, with the armour leading the way.

When the attack began, Rommel was at the front in the commander's tank of the leading

regiment. Leaving Sivry they went slowly on towards Clairfayts, which was avoided as the road was found to be mined. 'Suddenly we saw the angular outlines of a French fortification about 100 yards ahead.' Rommel recounts that the fully armed French standing by looked as if they were surrendering, but as fire was opened nearby they

A Panzer Mark III, carrying a 37mm gun and 3 machine-guns.

suddenly ran into the pillbox. It was then discovered that there was a deep anti-tank ditch in front of the pillbox and that the road from Clairfayts to Avesnes was blocked by steel hedgehogs. In the

Sd Kfz 251/1 Ausf A of 1st Infantry Regiment, 1 Panzer Division. Illustration by Bruce Culver.

meantime, 25th Panzer had attacked to the south of Clairfayts and the French artillery was bombarding both Sivry and Clairfayts. The German infantry and engineers, now covered by the fire from the tanks and their own artillery, began to penetrate the line of pillboxes. Opposite Rommel, where two tanks had already been knocked out, an engineer assault troop got forward and threw 6-pound demolition charges through the embrasure to force the garrison to surrender. As darkness fell, Rommel gave the order for an advance through the defence line with the intention of reaching Avesnes. 'The way to the west was now open. The moon was up and for the time being we could expect no real darkness. I had already given orders, in the plan for the breakthrough, for the leading tanks to scatter the road and verges with machine- and anti-tank gunfire at intervals during the drive to Avesnes, which I hoped would prevent the enemy from laying mines.' With the rest of the panzer regiment following closely and ready at any time to fire to either flank, the remainder of the division was ordered to follow up. With the divisional artillery firing on villages and the road well ahead, the drive forward started. Soon it reached a steady speed. Suddenly a gun opened up from the right of the road, but Rommel drove straight on while the tanks sprayed the cover on both sides. Soon the road became congested with all kinds of military vehicles as well as the carts of the refugees fleeing from the Germans. All was confusion, and Rommel's column slowed down to a crawl. Approaching Avesnes, Rommel made for some high ground to the west where he halted. 'Here, too, farmyards and orchards beside the road were jammed full of troops and refugee carts. All traffic down the road from the west was halted and picked up. Soon a prisoner-of-war cage had to be constructed in the field.' Then the sound of firing was heard in Avesnes – some French tanks had closed the road and the Germans were unable to shift them. The fighting started at about 0400 hours and lasted until dawn, when a Panzer IV sent by Rommel disposed of the remaining French tanks. Rommel had meanwhile continued the advance towards Landrecies with the 7th Motorcycle Battalion following. Some French were preparing to march off and Rommel's column came on them with

complete surprise. Nowhere was resistance offered, and the troops simply laid down their arms and moved off to the east. In Landrecies they came across a barracks full of French troops. An officer was sent in and the men were paraded and marched off as prisoners of war.

All this time Rommel had been trying to contact the division by wireless but had failed to do so. Believing that the division was close behind the column, he drove on to Le Cateau; here Rommel halted on a hill just to the east. He had advanced nearly 50 miles since the previous morning. His casualties over the two days came to one officer and less than forty other ranks; more than 10,000 prisoners were taken and more than a hundred tanks had been knocked out or captured. Of the French 1 Armoured Division, only three tanks crawled off the battlefield. Disaster had been met by many French units; the fates of 18 Division and 4 North African Division have already been mentioned: while 5 Motorized Division met its fate at Avesnes, and II Corps HQ was wiped out by a violent air attack. Furthermore, by capturing the bridge at Landrecies, the line Sambre-Oise, which General Georges had been determined to hold, had been breached.

17 May

Very early on 17 May, Guderian received a message from Armoured Group HQ that he must be on the airstrip at 0700 hours to meet General von Kleist and that any advance must be halted at once. The interview was quite extraordinary; von Kleist accused Guderian of having disobeyed orders – presumably some initiated by von Rundstedt the previous day about the panzers allowing the infantry protecting the flank to catch up. On Guderian asking to be relieved of his command, von Kleist seemed 'momentarily taken aback'. Then he ordered Guderian to hand over to General Veiel. Appalled, Guderian sent a signal to von Rundstedt that he was flying to Army Group HQ to report what had happened. Almost immediately the answer came back that Guderian must stay at his HQ and wait for General List, 'who has been instructed to clear the matter up'. Early that afternoon List arrived and asked what on earth was

Two French Hotchkiss tanks emerging from the edge of a wood.

going on. On von Rundstedt's orders Guderian was not to resign his command. Furthermore, the order on halting came from OKH and must be obeyed. For it was Hitler, urged on by von Rundstedt, who had got so worried about the southern flank being left 'unprotected'. List, however, persuaded von Rundstedt to agree that, while the Corps HQ must remain where it was, reconnaissance in force might be carried out. This was all that Guderian wanted: it allowed him the chance of getting his panzers moving again. All he had to do was to run a cable to his advanced HQ and issue orders without them going out by wireless.

By the evening the 'reconnaissance in force' was moving, with only the rear echelons held back. The pause that morning in the advance had given the panzers some rest and some time to carry out badly needed maintenance.

Also on 17 May, General Georges ordered co-ordinated attacks against the 'bulge' from both north and south. But only the attack from the south went in, made by 4 Armoured Division. This division, in the words of its commander, Colonel de Gaulle (appointed on 11 May), 'did not exist', as it was still assembling from very distant parts. Two days previously de Gaulle had been summoned by

Georges and told that Touchon was establishing a defensive front barring the route to Paris, and that 4 Armoured Division would gain time for Touchon. So de Gaulle went off to Laon where he met an embryo staff. He carried out a reconnaissance and decided to strike with whatever was available at Montcornet on 17 May. The three battalions of tanks that had assembled there were the 46th 'B' tank Battalion and two battalions of light Renault R-35s with the obsolete short-range 37mm gun. In addition, there was a company of the D2 (16 ton) infantry tanks with the powerful 47mm gun, and a battalion of 4th Chasseurs transported in buses, but with no proper anti-aircraft weapons.

At first light on 17 May de Gaulle set out. To begin with all went well: a German reconnaissance column was shot up; two armoured cars were destroyed and then another line of soft vehicles were left on fire. By 1500 hours de Gaulle's tanks had fought their way into Montcornet. Here and at Lislet the fighting continued with the Germans gradually getting the upper hand. In the evening the

French tanks had turned back. Low in petrol and without the direct support of the infantry, they could do nothing else. De Gaulle gives his own estimate of the attack; it had left '... several hundred German dead and plenty of burned-out lorries on the field. We had taken 130 prisoners. We had lost less than two hundred men.' But as Alistair Horne writes, '... it could hardly be described as anything more than an armoured raid of ephemeral consequence'.

Elsewhere on the northern part of the bulge, General Georges' attempt to mount a counter-attack failed miserably. The advance of the panzers during the previous twenty-four hours had seized many of the points on which Georges had placed

such store; and French units everywhere remained on the defensive.

Rommel had discovered early on 17 May that only a few of the panzer regiments and some of the motorcycle regiment had been following him the night before. Thinking that the rest of the division were close behind, he set off to bring them up. Motoring back, he kept on meeting bodies of French troops who only seemed to be waiting to be rounded-up. Outside Avesnes he ran into a convoy of French troops which suddenly emerged from a side road. 'At our shouts it halted and a French officer got out and surrendered.' In the swirling dust he then led the convoy into Avesnes where the rest of 7 Panzer Division was beginning to arrive.

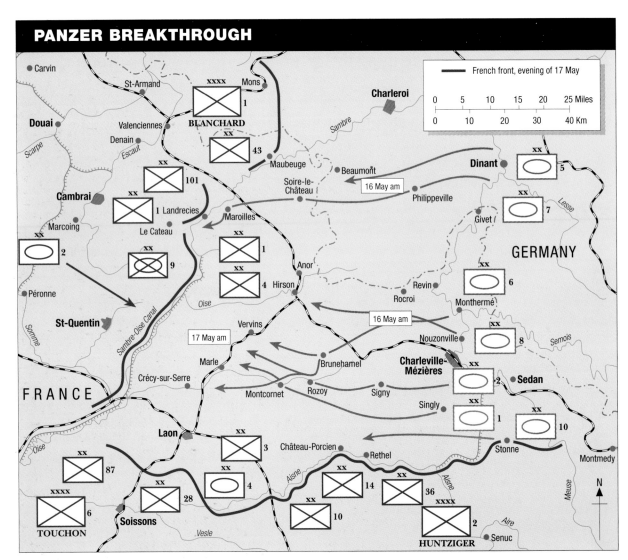

PANZER BREAKTHROUGH

On Reinhardt's front, 8 Panzer Division had reached the upper Oise south of La Capelle, while tanks of 6 Panzer Division had seized a bridge at Origny before the order to halt had been received. At the same time 1 Panzer Division had captured Ribemont and Crécy-sur-Serre, while the 'reconnaissance in force' had enabled Guderian to establish a number of bridgeheads over Georges' river barrier.

The General Scene: 16 and 17 May

Up to the evening of 15 May the French High Command had failed to believe that the panzers had broken through at Sedan. Then that evening Gamelin phoned Daladier with the news of the German advances in the south. At about the same time Georges at la Ferté got the first news of Reinhardt's panzers having reached Montcornet. For the French High Command the whole scene was totally transformed. Paris itself was more directly threatened in their minds. At 1745 on 14 May, Reynaud had sent an urgent message to Churchill telling him that the Germans had 'broken through our fortified lines south of Sedan'. Reynaud needed more fighters to isolate the panzers from their supporting Stukas. It was essential that Churchill send additional squadrons.

*German infantry firing a
light machine-gun.*

Then early the following morning, 15 May, Reynaud telephoned Churchill who was still in bed: 'We have been defeated – we are beaten; we have lost the battle.' Churchill tried to calm him and finally said that he would come to Paris to see Reynaud, and on the afternoon of 16 May he flew over accompanied by Generals Ismay and Dill. Just before he left, four extra fighter squadrons were standing by to leave England for France. Churchill's trip to cheer up the French government did little to achieve that result – it certainly gave Ismay and Dill the chance of seeing what was likely to happen. So when the party returned, action was taken to encourage the French at the same time as retrenchment at home. As regards the ten squadrons that had been promised to France, it was decided that they should operate from the south of England. In France this decision was the cause of bitter disappointment. Meanwhile both Gamelin and Georges were still deluded as to the German's goal – it must be Paris! No real thought was given to von Rundstedt's making for the coast and cutting off the Allied armies in the north.

Reynaud had meanwhile sent a telegram to General Weygand who was commanding in the Levant. He was to come to Paris at once, and the message ended '...secrecy of your departure desirable'. The same day, travelling by night train to Madrid, was a special envoy recalling Marshal Pétain.

The 17 May was also the day when the German infantry regiments were catching up and moving to guard the flank of the panzers' advance. For days they had been marching, ever marching in the heat and dust. Little or no motorized transport was ever available, and their supplies came up by horse-drawn carts. The German engineers were also busy repairing the railways and soon would reach Dinant.

The Luftwaffe too were getting their bases forward – leapfrogging in turn to get the squadrons close behind the panzers. Here the ubiquitous Ju 52 transport aircraft was of prime importance. Everything needed – ammunition, spares, crews and petrol – all was brought up and dumped as soon as an airfield had been captured. By comparison, the Allied air effort had been reduced by the AASF

Refugees, their carts piled high, moving back on every road.

withdrawal from its advanced bases. The French were crippled by casualties and the weakness of their supply organization, where for instance depots closed down on Sundays and after hours, and operational pilots had to travel back to fetch replacement aircraft.

18 to 23 May

At dawn on 18 May the panzers were again on the move. Guderian's 2 Panzer Division took St-Quentin by 0800, while on the left 1 Panzer Division was over the Somme by noon; 10 Panzer was also advancing, blocking any interference from the southern flank. Further north, 6 Panzer Division was engaged in heavy fighting near le Catelet against French 'B' tanks. Eventually, however, this last section of the French 2 Armoured Division was overcome and the Germans had captured the nearby Headquarters of Ninth Army. Rommel was involved in fighting between Landrecies and le Cateau where part of his force was waiting for petrol and ammunition. Here he eventually won through by midday, and then advanced on Cambrai with only a few tanks

and some flak guns, plus a composite battalion of motorized infantry. This drummed-up force swept towards the town on a broad front and created such a cloud of dust that the French thought it was a major tank attack. By nightfall the town had been taken. On an airfield near Cambrai were forty-two aircraft that had been shot up on the ground by the Luftwaffe.

Meanwhile Touchon's force formed behind the Aisne to guard against an attack on Paris! While a newly constituted Seventh Army under General Frère got to the canal between Ham and la Fère and then had to dig in, all that remained between the panzers and the sea were two half-strength British Territorial divisions, 12 and 23 Divisions, which had been in France for a month on line of communications duties. The following day General Giraud was captured by the advancing Germans; his command had lasted exactly three and a half days.

The Allies were encumbered by the refugees on the roads. Not only were reinforcements held up, but the wounded were trapped in ambulances in

A German motorcycle reconnaissance unit.

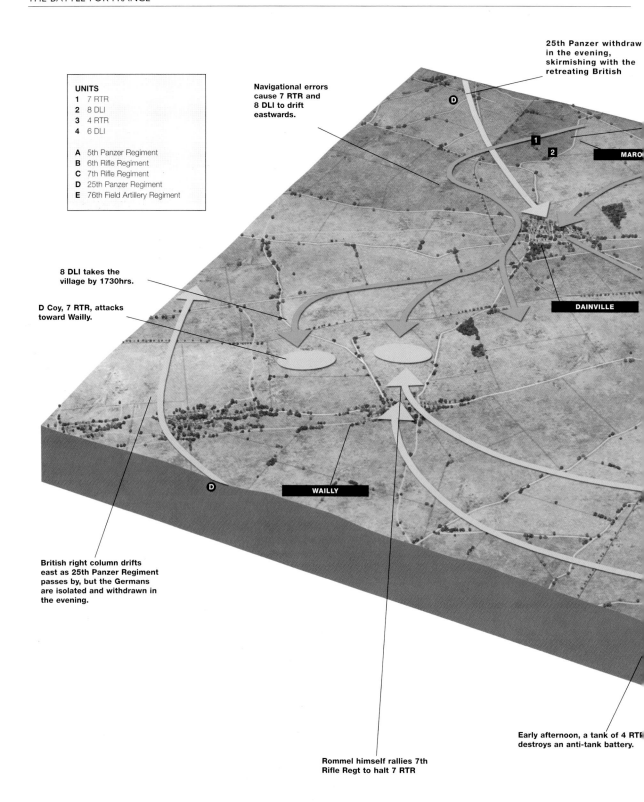

UNITS
1 7 RTR
2 8 DLI
3 4 RTR
4 6 DLI

A 5th Panzer Regiment
B 6th Rifle Regiment
C 7th Rifle Regiment
D 25th Panzer Regiment
E 76th Field Artillery Regiment

Navigational errors
cause 7 RTR and
8 DLI to drift
eastwards.

25th Panzer withdraw
in the evening,
skirmishing with the
retreating British

MARO

DAINVILLE

8 DLI takes the
village by 1730hrs.

D Coy, 7 RTR, attacks
toward Wailly.

WAILLY

British right column drifts
east as 25th Panzer Regiment
passes by, but the Germans
are isolated and withdrawn in
the evening.

Early afternoon, a tank of 4 RTR
destroys an anti-tank battery.

Rommel himself rallies 7th
Rifle Regt to halt 7 RTR

THE ARRAS COUNTERATTACK, 21 MAY 1940

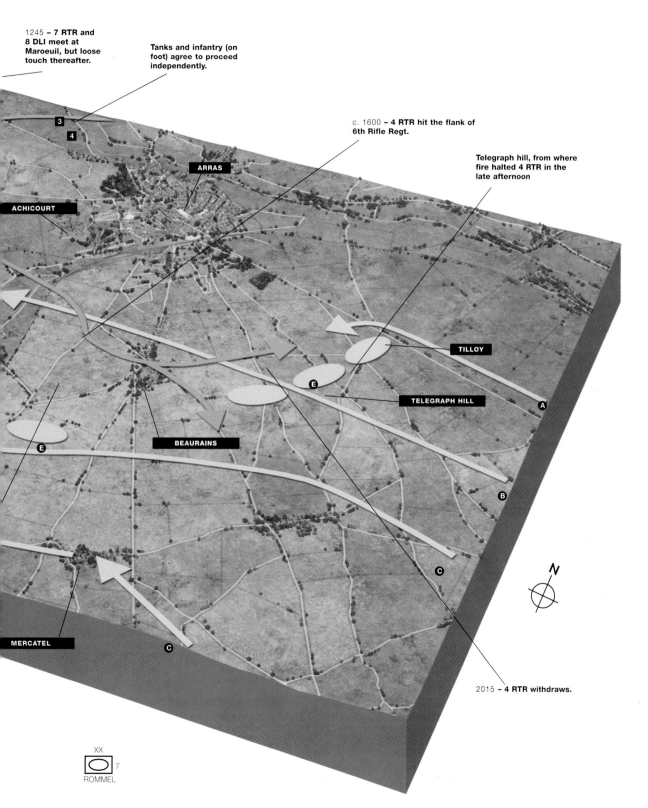

1245 – **7 RTR** and **8 DLI** meet at Maroeuil, but loose touch thereafter.

Tanks and infantry (on foot) agree to proceed independently.

3
4

ARRAS

ACHICOURT

c. 1600 – **4 RTR** hit the flank of 6th Rifle Regt.

Telegraph hill, from where fire halted **4 RTR** in the late afternoon

TILLOY

E

TELEGRAPH HILL

A

BEAURAINS

E

B

C

C

MERCATEL

C

2015 – **4 RTR** withdraws.

N

XX
7
ROMMEL

traffic blocks. Earlier the BEF had operated a scheme for evacuating 800,000 inhabitants from the industrial areas of northern France. Many were now trying to force their way back, having run into the panzers, or been frightened by rumours of the armoured column. 'Like one big wave, the whole of this humanity, short of food and sleep and terrified to the core, was now surging back again and congesting all roads at a moment when mobility was a vital element.'

To attack Guderian's line of advance, de Gaulle on 19 May struck north towards Crécy. His armoured force now totalled 150 tanks. Thirty were 'B' tanks and forty were Somuas or D2s. He also had a battalion of infantry and a regiment of 75mms. At first de Gaulle made good progress and reached the Serre in four hours. But here the opposition had been organized by Guderian, and Crécy was 'a fortress of anti-tank guns, an enormous ambush'. De Gaulle's light tanks were seriously repulsed. The D2s now went in but suffered casualties – and as the infantry had failed

Renault tank halted with German troops, temporarily stopping in a village.

to appear the attack was eventually called off by General Georges. The real trouble had been the failure of d'Astier to hold off the Stukas, as the time of the attack had been changed and d'Astier had not been told.

By the end of 19 May all of Hitler's panzers, except 9 Panzer Division, were lined-up some fifty miles from the sea ready for the final advance. That day General Gort was warning the British War Office that it might have to consider evacuating the BEF, and the War Office and Admiralty began discussions, under the code-name 'Dynamo', of achieving this possible operation.

That night Gamelin was replaced by Weygand.

The Allies were now behind the Escaut, on the left of the Belgians; then came the BEF and First Army, with 50 Division (of BEF), less a brigade group, on Vimy Ridge around Arras.

On 20 May, Guderian started off at 0400 hours. Balck's tanks reached Amiens, thirty-five miles away, by mid-morning. Here they met the men of the Royal Sussex Regiment who fought to the finish, the battalion being wiped out. Meanwhile 2 Panzer Division was advancing on Abbeville, where it engaged the remnants of the British 35 Brigade which had fallen back across the Somme.

French prisoners of war passing through a bombed village.

Reinhardt's division first met the British at Mondicourt and eventually broke through. Later at Doullens they confronted the outnumbered men of 36 Brigade who held out until darkness was falling. By the end of 20 May the two British Territorial divisions, fighting against impossible odds, had been wiped out. As for Rommel, the day had not gone so well as he had been held up by the British at Arras where he was forced on to the defensive. Nevertheless 20 May brought Guderian his triumph: part of Lieutenant-Colonel Spitta's battalion of 2 Panzer Division reached the coast near Noyelles, having advanced more than sixty miles. It was a truly remarkable achievement.

On the previous day General Ironside had arrived to persuade Gort to move south to join up with the French. Gort, however, refused as nine divisions were engaged on the Escault and he would not abandon the Belgians. He mentioned the plans for a limited attack from Arras on 21 May. Hearing that Gort had not received any orders from Billotte for eight days, Ironside left for Billotte's HQ. Here he found Billotte with Blanchard, both in a state of complete depression. Ironside lost his temper and persuaded the two French generals to agree to join the British attack with two divisions. After Ironside had left for London, Gort told his Liaison Officer to warn both Billotte and Blanchard that if the attack failed both '... the French and British Armies north of the gap would have their flank turned and could no longer remain in their present positions'.

At the Headquarters of Major-General Franklyn there was no representative of Altmayer's V Corps, and late that night a letter arrived from Blanchard saying that General Altmayer could not move for two days as 'the roads were so badly blocked', but that General Prioux would cover the western flank of the attack. Prioux's problems were mounting, however, as most of 1 Light Mechanized Division's tanks had been lost, and he could not extract his own tanks from the infantry divisions. Meanwhile General Georges had not given d'Astier any details of the time of the attack, only asking for 'powerful support'. So the attack went in with two mobile columns, each of a tank battalion and an infantry battalion, plus a battery of field guns and an anti-tank battery – but with no air support at all. The British right column took Duisans but had to leave two companies and some anti-tank guns to hold the village. Taking Warlus against strong opposition, the column pushed on to Wailly where it ran into Rommel's 7th Rifle Regiment. Here intense fighting eventually resulted in the column's withdrawal to Warlus.

The British left-hand column made good progress. Advancing through Dainville, the tanks broke up a motorized column and took a number of prisoners. Then the Matildas overran a German anti-tank battery near Achicourt. Around Agny and Beaurains the heavy British tanks and Rommel's 6 Rifle Regiment backed by artillery fought a very heavy action. But there were no British troops to follow up. Meanwhile the British 50 Division had

made a harassing raid towards Tilloy and also 13 Brigade had established a bridgehead further east in preparation for the second day. But, unable to hold the ground and with his rear threatened, Franklyn called off the attack. He had advanced ten miles and taken four hundred prisoners; but his losses included all but twenty-six of the Mark I tank and two valuable Mark II tanks.

Rommel's subsequent remarks about this action are worth recording. 'The anti-tank guns which we quickly deployed showed themselves to be far too light to be effective against the heavily armoured British tanks, and the majority of them were put out of action by gunfire, together with their crews, and then overrun by the enemy tanks. Many of our vehicles were burnt out. SS units close by also had to fall back to the south before the weight of the tank attack.' The official history of 7 Panzer Division gives the manpower losses on that day as 378, four times the losses suffered in the break-through into France. That evening Rommel attacked north-west of Arras. In a sharp engagement seven more of the British heavy tanks were knocked out. But the Germans had lost far more tanks than in any operation so far. The failure

Major-General G. le Q. Martel, GOC 50 Division, BEF, a recognized authority on tank warfare.

of the British attack, however, convinced Gort that the BEF should fall back on Dunkirk.

Weygand flew north to visit Billotte, Gort and King Leopold on 21 May. Landing at Calais he discovered that the King was at Ypres. Eventually Weygand arrived there and spent several abortive hours trying to persuade the King to withdraw the Belgian Army to the Yser. This would have allowed the BEF to concentrate so as to strike south, while the French attacked north from the Somme. Billotte then arrived and pointed out the confused state of First Army. After waiting for Gort until 1900 hours, Weygand left. Owing to the bombing he could not fly and he eventually reached Paris at 1000 hours on 22 May via Dover and Cherbourg. Gort arrived at Ypres shortly after Weygand had left, never having received the message about the meeting. Billotte told him of Weygand's intentions,

THE RACE TO THE SEA

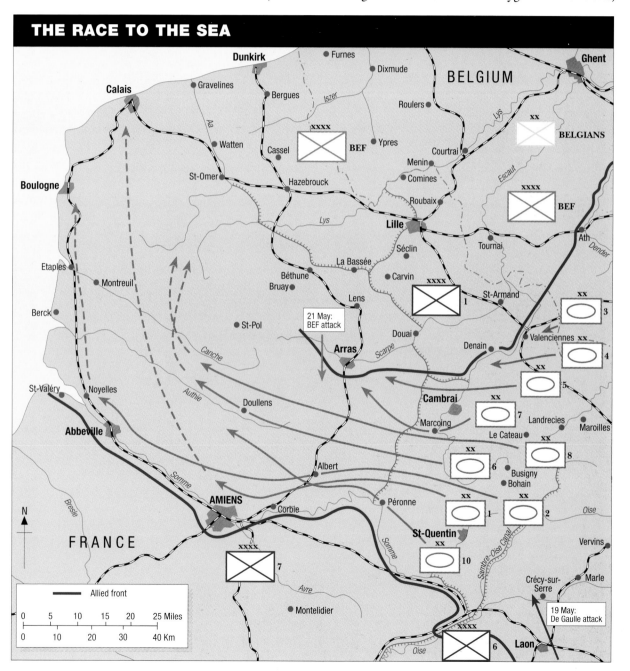

A French light Renault Ft18 tank, captured by the Germans, in Rouen.

French refugees slowly returning home. Unarmed French soldiers can clearly be seen in the walking party.

but Gort considered that he could not make the changes for the attack before 26 May.

That night Billotte's car taking him to see Blanchard skidded into the back of a lorry carrying refugees. Billotte was seriously injured and, after two days in a coma, died. This was a most serious blow to the Allies, as he was the only one who knew Weygand's plans at first-hand. Meanwhile three days passed before Blanchard was moved up, while Prioux moved to take over First Army, during which time there was no co-ordination to the 'Weygand Plan'.

Early on 22 May, Guderian moved forward to seize the Channel ports: 1 Panzer Division and Grossdeutschland were to go for Calais, while 2 Panzer Division went for Boulogne. That afternoon the approaches to Boulogne were furiously contested, but by the evening both divisions were on the outskirts of their objectives. Overnight 10 Panzer Division was moved up and replaced 1 Panzer, which was sent towards Dunkirk, but was halted on the Aa Canal. Boulogne held out until 25 May, defended by the Irish and Welsh Guards, while Brigadier Nicholson held on at Calais until 26 May, a fine action by the Rifle Brigade which pinned down 10 Panzer Division.

Meanwhile General Altmayer had launched his attack with only one infantry regiment, the 121st, and supported by artillery and two armoured reconnaissance groups. It started to the east of Douai and the light tanks quickly got to the outskirts of Cambrai. Here it administered a hard blow to the German 32 Infantry Division, but was bombed by Henschel 123s and cannon-firing Messerschmitts. Finally, it was halted by the 88mms firing at only 150 yards' range. Gort had not been told about the attack, nor had he received any orders about the 'Weygand Plan', so he sent a telegram to the British Secretary of State for War, indicating the lack of co-ordination between the three armies and asking for Sir John Dill to fly out to make an on-the-spot appreciation. To Eden he bluntly pointed out that he had insufficient ammunition for a second attack and that relief must come from the south.

In the early hours of 23 May, Gort withdrew 'Frankforce' and during the night the British 5 and 50 Divisions moved back some fifteen miles to behind the Haute Deule Canal, north-east of Arras. This was a very necessary decision, which Gort made himself, but it was one that aroused deep feelings among the French. He had accepted that the French Army was finished and that it was his simple duty to save the BEF in order to continue the war.

Dunkirk

The following day, 24 May, an event occurred that was to have dramatic consequences. Early that day both Guderian and Reinhardt had forced bridge-heads over the Aa Canal and were about to press on to Dunkirk. Then an order came that the whole of the left wing should halt on the line of the canal. Dunkirk was to be left to the Luftwaffe and Army Group B. This partly resulted from Goering's call on the telephone to Hitler the previous day and partly from a fear of the boggy terrain. The next day Hitler went to von Rundstedt's HQ at Charleville. Von Rundstedt wanted to keep the panzers for the forthcoming battle south of the Somme and agreed to halting them on the Aa Canal. It was three days before Hitler changed his mind and allowed the panzers to continue the advance. But at that very moment the first evacuation from Dunkirk was starting. The defence perimeter had been strengthened and in Britain the fleet of boats was assembling. This day, 26 May, Gort received an instruction 'to operate towards the coast forthwith'. But few thought that many of his troops would get away.

Rommel with the tanks of 5 Panzer Division under command had a hard fight to cross the la Bassée Canal east of Béthune, which was held by the British. 5 Panzer Division then went forward to capture Armentières, while Rommel went eastwards to meet the German infantry. Near Lille, General Molinié fought an immensely courageous action for four more days with a pocket of troops from First Army. This bravery enabled the remainder of First Army to fall back into the Dunkirk perimeter. Guderian had reached Gravelines on the coast by 29 May; then orders came that his whole corps, together with 7 Panzer Division was to withdraw for Operation 'Red' in the south.

On 27 May the long-awaited attack from the south by the French took place. Under General Grandsard, the 7 and 4 Colonial Infantry Divisions backed by a few Somuas attacked towards Amiens. They got within sight of the city and caused the Germans some anxiety but were finally thrown back to their start-line. The following day de Gaulle had his third action and was supported by the British 51 (Highland) Division. He was attacking the German bridgehead around Abbeville. Writing later, de Gaulle claimed that five hundred German prisoners had been captured; but on the second day the attack halted and was driven back. The German bridgehead had not been captured and the panzer

A Lockheed Hudson of RAF Coastal Command flying on reconnaissance patrol near Dunkirk, where the acrid fumes of burning oil tanks billow upward.

corridor was not broken. Early that morning the surrender of the Belgian Army was made known; inevitable as it was, the news was received with much anger throughout France.

Meanwhile the evacuation at Dunkirk had started. By 27 May only 7,669 troops had left, but the next day, the Royal Navy being reinforced by an armada of small boats, the figure was 17,804. On 29 May, with the arrival of a French warship, 47,310 men were evacuated, with a peak of 68,014 on 31 May. No orders came for the French to evacuate until 29 May, after which Churchill gave orders that an equal allocation should be observed. By the morning of 3 June the last British troops had left and the Germans were only a mile and a half from the sea. At dawn on 4 June the last ship left, laden with French troops. But some 30,000 French soldiers had to be left behind. Nevertheless the final figure of 338,226 men, of whom 198,315 were

LAST DAYS

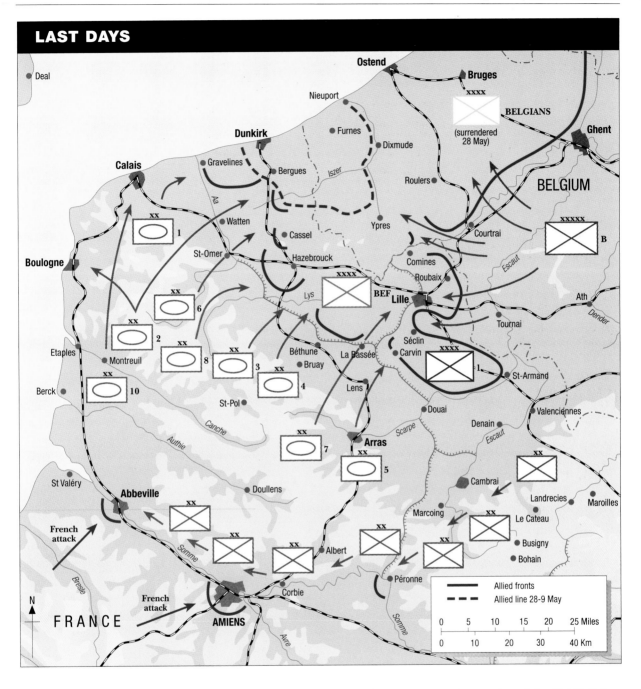

British had been saved. The cost in ships was six British and two French destroyers and many smaller craft. The success of the evacuation had largely been made possible by the RAF assisted by a change in the weather. On at least half of the days involved this change seriously affected the Luftwaffe in their attempts to 'finish the job', as Goering had promised. On the good weather days the Luftwaffe, weakened by their losses, had to

contend with the whole weight of the RAF flying from nearby bases across the Straits of Dover. During the whole period the British fighters flew 2,739 sorties, with many pilots flying four in a day. To the French, Dunkirk was a defeat and the desertion of an ally; to the British it will always be seen as a great triumph. As Alistair Horne writes, 'it was Hitler who in terms of overall war strategy, suffered the most injurious defeat at Dunkirk.'

THE RESULT

Casualties can give some indication of what happened. These have been taken from Alastair Horne's *To Lose a Battle*, and he makes it clear that the French losses are probably underestimated. The German casualties were 156,492 (killed 27,074; wounded 111,034; missing 18,384). French losses were estimated as 2,190,000 (killed 90,000; wounded 200,000; missing/prisoners 1,900,000). Other Allied losses were more modest: British 68,111, Belgian 23,350 and Dutch 9,779. Given the fact that after the armistice Germany progressively 'milked' the manhood of France for slave labour, the true extent of the French defeat can be seen. It is also true to say that Hitler's belief in his own infallibility had been considerably strengthened. So what subsequently went wrong for Hitler?

Hitler's greatest mistake was in no way connected with the brilliant '*Sichelschnitt*' plan; it was simply that he had made no plans beyond the defeat of France. Nor, indeed, had he in fact directed the 'cut of the sickle' to swing westwards

The heartbreaking side of evacuation. The burning lorries show this all too clearly, as the BEF had to destroy their heavy equipment before they left Dunkirk.

Before the Armistice. The rear entrance of the armoured Fort No. 505, stormed by 71 Division in 1940. This fort formed part of the main defensive positions of the Maginot Line.

British and French prisoners of war in the harbour at Dunkirk – a German photograph.

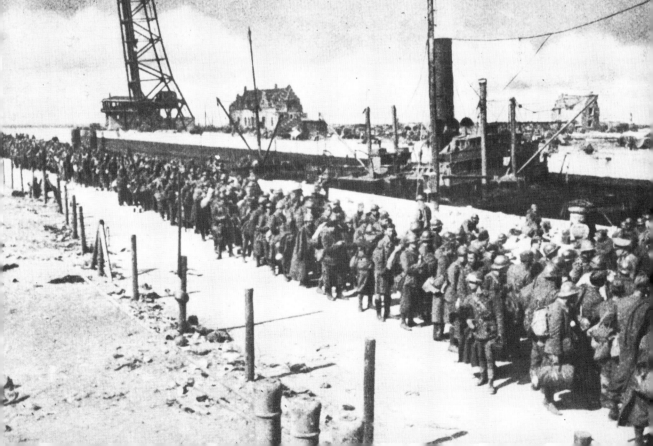

March past of German troops on the Place de la Concorde in Paris, 14 June 1940.

Hitler, in festive mood, shows his delight before the signing of the French Armistice, 22 June 1940.

and surround the Allied armies in the north. For, when Guderian broke through and threatened his opponents in three different directions, it was he who made that decision. Again, when the Panzers reached the sea and the British Expeditionary Force began to withdraw on Dunkirk, Hitler's decision to save his panzers from the mud and allow infantry and aircraft to finish the job gave Gort time to get most of the BEF safely back to England. With no immediate plans to follow up the defeat of France and invade Britain, as each day passed this opportunity was lost and never regained by Germany. So long as Britain remained in the war, then was it not inevitable that the United States would eventually join her in the fight for freedom from Germany's iron grip on Europe?

The German 'Sichelschnitt' had been a brilliant success – a plan that in a matter of days had brought France to a humiliating defeat – but in the end it was Hitler's lack of forethought that finally led him into a prolonged war and defeat for Germany itself.

Just after the Armistice. A German Pz Kpfw III passing through a devastated French village on the River Aisne on 12 July 1940. The French had been forced to agree to an armistice on 22 June.

CHRONOLOGY

1935 Hitler announces creation of Luftwaffe, which already has 1,000 front-line aircraft.

1936 Hitler speeds up manufacture of light and medium bombers.

1937 Germany has 39 divisions in her army.

March 1938 *Anschluss*: annexation of Austria.

October Repossession of Sudetenland.

January 1939 German Army strength now 51 divisions.

March Invasion of Czechoslovakia.

May Germany signs Pact of Steel with Italy.

August Germany signs Non-Aggression Pact with Russia.

1 September Invasion of Poland.

3 September Britain and France declare war on Germany; on mobilization Germany fields more than 100 divisions.

10 September British Expeditionary Force established in Northern France.

10 January German courier carrying plans for invasion of Holland and Belgium arrested on Belgian territory.

February German Plan 'Sichelschnitt' eventually emerges, giving main attack to von Rundstedt (45 divisions including 7 panzer divisions) through Ardennes on front Dinant to Sedan; von Bock in the north (with 29 divisions including 3 panzer divisions) to draw and hold the Allies; von Leeb (19 divisions) in the south opposite the Maginot Line to prevent French reinforcements moving up.

March Gamelin adopts Dyle-Breda Plan to strengthen the Allied left flank.

9 April Germany invades Norway.

9 May Chamberlain resigns British premiership. German 'tourists' cross frontiers ready to seize road junctions. Hitler orders assault on France to open overnight.

10 May Specially trained troops in gliders land on Belgian forts at Eben Emael. German advance starts before dawn, with paratroops attacking bridge across Maas estuary. Luftwaffe opens offensive deep into France. British Expeditionary Force and French cavalry move to Dyle Line. French Cavalry in centre advance. Allied air effort frustrated by orders 'to avoid built-up areas'. Churchill takes up British premiership.

11 May In the centre, Guderian reaches River Semois and crosses during the night. In the north, Prioux with French cavalry has difficulty in reaching new positions. Georges makes plans to move reinforcements behind Sedan, but it is already too late. Meanwhile the Dutch air force is virtually impotent.

12 May In the north the Germans reach Zuider Zee, and the French are forced to withdraw to cover Antwerp. Belgians pull back. In the centre, Rommel reaches Houx before night and crosses the Meuse. D'Astier draws attention to the German advance between Dinant and Bouillon. Guderian reaches east bank of Meuse at Sedan.

13 May Rommel increases pressure at Houx and crosses at Dinant. Boucher orders French counter-attacks, which fail. Stuka support around Sedan terrifies French. The Grossdeutschland Regiment crosses near Gaulier and reaches la Marfée heights. 10 Panzer division's assault engineers eventually cross near Wadelincourt. Panic and false reports spread among, French troops and refugees pour southwards.

14 May Colonel Balck reaches Chéhéry with 1 Rifle Regiment. Reinhardt's corps, held for two days, finally forces a partial crossing at Monthermé. In the Netherlands, Prioux's cavalry stand ground against the panzers but withdraw at night after heavy losses. Georges at last accepts the fact of German success at Sedan. Rommel reaches Onhaye. German infantry divisions cross at Nouzonville at the third attempt. French attacks with tanks near Bulson fail. Guderian wheels westward, leaving 10 Panzer Division and the

Grossdeutschland regiment to hold the flank. French 3 Armoured Division attack is cancelled. Huntziger and Corap make wrong appreciation and open the way for German advance. Fierce air battle over Sedan with very heavy RAF losses. Rotterdam bombed by Germans during cease-fire negotiations. Netherlands capitulates.

15 May Rommel continues advance towards Philippeville. 6 Panzer Division at Monthermé manages to cross in strength. At Stonne fierce fighting eventually leaves German Grossdeutschland in command. 1 and 2 Panzer Divisions finally break through Touchon's force. Corap is removed and replaced by Giraud.

16 May Guderian's panzers advance 40 miles in the day. French 2 Armoured Division still scattered. Rommel breaks through remnants of XI Corps and makes for Le Cateau.

17 May Guderian's advance is halted by the High Command but finally allowed a 'reconnaissance in force'. De Gaulle attacks with 4 Armoured Division, reaching Montcornet, but turns back at nightfall.

18 May Panzers ordered to continue advance. Rommel takes Cambrai with scratch force. Refugees hamper all movement on roads.

19 May De Gaulle makes abortive attack with tanks and infantry towards Crécy. D'Astier fails to hold off Stukas. Weygand replaces Gamelin. Panzers in line for final advance about 50 miles from the sea.

20 May Royal Sussex Regiment fight to the end at Amiens, and Panzers wipe out two British Territorial Army divisions. Part of 2 Panzer Division reaches the sea near Noyelles. Ironside persuades French to take part in joint attack with BEF towards Amiens on 21 May.

21 May French fail to produce troops or air support for joint attack. Two British columns of tanks and infantry fight a fierce action south of Arras but are eventually forced to retire.

22 May Panzers drive for the Channel ports. French (Altmayer) attack makes initial success but is eventually halted. Gort still without orders.

23 May Decision by Gort to save BEF.

24 May Reynaud complains to Churchill over British withdrawal. Hitler orders panzers to halt at Aa Canal, giving BEF vital time.

26 May German tanks again advance on Dunkirk.

27 May Evacuation of BEF starts.

28 May Belgium surrenders.

29 May French join in evacuation.

4 June BEF and French evacuation ends.

5–22 June Between the sea and the Meuse, Germany launches a fresh attack with 104 fully manned divisions against the French, who now have only 60 divisions and very weak air cover. Although the French fight with great courage, the Germans take Paris on 14 June and have reached a line from Bordeaux to the Swiss frontier by the time the armistice is signed on 22 June.

A GUIDE TO FURTHER READING

Benoist-Méchin, J., *Sixty Days that Shook the West*, (London, 1963)

Bond, Brian, *Britain, France and Belgium 1939-1940*, (London, 1990)

Churchill, Winston S., *The Second World War Volume II: Their Finest Hour*, (London, 1949)

Deighton, Len, *Blitzkrieg*, (London, 1979)

Guderian, Heinz, *Panzer Leader*, (London, 2000)

Horne, Alistair, *To Lose a Battle, France 1940*, (London, 1990)

Jacobsen, Hans-Adolf and Jürgen Rohwer, *Decisive Battles of World War II: the German View*, (London, 1965)

Marix Evans, Martin, *The Fall of France: Act with Daring*, (Oxford, 2000)

Rommel, Erwin, ed. B. H. Liddell Hart, *The Rommel Papers*, (London, 1953)

WARGAMING FRANCE 1940

The battles of May 1940 have much to commend them to the wargamer. The short campaign is packed with heroic last stands, river assaults, armour clashes and desperate counter-attacks. For the more inquisitive mind there are no shortage of 'What if?'s.

Several sets of rules are available for the period, but most attempt a broad general coverage of Second World War situations. Some wargamers derive satisfaction in designing their own rules to fit a particular campaign. To create an accurate feel of a 1940 game one has to have regard to the tactics used by the combatants and technological limitations of the equipment they used. Nowhere is this more evident than in the design and use of the tank.

French tanks were often equal to, and in many cases, superior to, German machines; it was in the areas of command, organization and tactics that the Germans excelled. Most French designs had poor or no radio communication facilities. Their main anti-tank weapon was often housed in a single-man turret operated by the vehicle commander so that, in addition to directing the driver and other members of the crew, a French tank commander was also required to select targets and load and fire the gun. In his spare time he could attempt to discover what other vehicles in the troop were doing. The majority of German tanks, however, often had well designed, three-man turrets which left the commander free to carry out his primary role without burdening him with other duties. A failing of many sets of wargame rules is that they permit French tanks to operate as efficiently as their enemy.

In May 1940 tanks ruled the battlefield. Never again would they inspire the same widespread brain-numbing fear they caused as they chased across the plains of France. The lightning thrust through the Ardennes to the coast was largely achieved by fast-moving panzer divisions to which

the Allies did not have an effective answer. Wargamers should remember, however, that the Germans did not hold a monopoly in 'tank terror'. At Arras, German infantry from the 6th Rifle Regiment fled in panic when they saw 37mm shells bouncing off the Matildas of the 4th Royal Tank Regiment. Rules should not make the Germans into supermen but give them tactical advantages for their flexibility and organizational skill.

The invasion of France can be wargamed as one campaign (a daunting task) or broken down into more manageable components such as a series of 'mini campaigns'. The assault on the Meuse between Houx and Dinant and De Gaulle's 4th DCR counter-attack of 17/19 May are two examples. Any wargames campaign would not necessarily require as much logistical planning as those staged in other Second World War theatres. Nor was there a 'scorched earth' policy in 1940 France: German tanks were fitted with petrol engines and were able to fill up at roadside petrol stations when they outran their own supply lines.

Thorough reconnaissance was important to the success of this style of warfare. German reconnaissance units probed forward ahead of the panzers to find the point of least resistance. The main armoured thrust, or *Schwerpunkt*, would then be made at this point to effect a breakthrough. Strongpoints would be bypassed and left for the following infantry formations to deal with. Each panzer division had its own reconnaissance battalion (Aufklarungs Abteilung). These were well balanced units and were capable of independent action. Armour was provided by a combination of light and heavy armoured cars and radio vehicles. (Often there was also an air liaison officer to direct the dreaded Stukas.) The battalion's infantry were normally motorized on motor-cycle combinations and were supported by mortars, light howitzers and anti-tank guns. In an advance the armoured cars generally scouted the main roads while the fast-moving motor-cycle units explored the minor roads and lanes.

This 'probing' concept may be used in a wargames campaign. An umpire could allocate the Allied commander insufficient forces to cover a vital area of the front in any depth (a situation that existed at Sedan). After his dispositions are marked on a map, the German commander's task would be to seek out the weak point(s) in the front. Reconnaissance units would advance using map movement until the umpire determined a contact had been made. The action could then be transferred to the table top, with Germans attempting to draw fire to assess the levels of resistance.

In moderating a multi-player campaign, such as that played by a club, an umpire may wish to simulate the shortcomings of the Allied command structure (preferably headstrong in the case of the French) and they should be permitted only limited contact with each other.

In terms of scale, today's wargamer is spoilt for choice; models and figures are available in 2, 6, 15, 20 and 54mm scales as well in the increasingly popular 1/200th ranges. Vehicles, aircraft and infantry in white metal are readily available in the smaller scales from several manufacturers. 20mm vehicles present more of a problem as most plastic construction kits are of late war designs. However, the specialist cast-resin firms are rapidly filling the gaps. Details of such firms can be found from time to time in modelling magazines, and the products can be obtained either by mail order or from stands at wargames conventions. The BEF in particular went to war in many commandeered civilian vehicles. Several suitable examples can be found by rummaging through the railway accessories at the local model shop.

The choice of scale is, to a certain extent, influenced by the type of engagement the gamer is trying to recreate. The smaller scales lend themselves more readily to the larger battles, especially if significant numbers of tanks or more than about a company of infantry are involved. Questions of scale are not confined to the size of the models but include the representation of units on the table top. Most commercial rules for the period adopt a 1:1 ratio. In other words, a model figure or vehicle is what it appears to be on the table and does not represent a larger body of troops. A different approach was used by one of the 'greats' in Second World War wargaming, the late John Sanders. This was to scale down unit sizes representing, say, a battalion with a nominal strength of 500, to approximately 20 miniature figures. Similarly a company of tanks appears as only two or three models. This is the system also employed in the popular American *Command Decision* rules and allows relatively large actions to be refought in 20mm scale.

Historical accounts of the engagements in the campaign can provide a basis for game design and a little research can produce a very enjoyable "bash". One such account, which provided the inspiration for one of my games, appeared in the 4 October 1940 edition of *The War Illustrated* and was entitled 'When the R.H.A. Stood at Bay at Hondeghem'. The opening paragraph of the article (which was basically an exercise in propaganda) read: 'Of all the close range fighting between British and German troops in France during the last few days of May 1940 there was no more gallantly contested engagement than that of the defence of Hondeghem village by "K" Battery of the Royal Horse Artillery.'

On 26 May, 1940 German forces were in full flood along the main road from St-Omer to Mt. Cassel in their thrust to the Channel ports. The village of Hondeghem stood in the direct line of the enemy advance. The task of delaying this advance was allotted to four 18-pounder guns of 'K' Battery, RHA. No regular infantry were available, but 80 men and one officer of a searchlight unit were scraped together to bolster the defences. The German attack began in earnest at 7.30am on 27 May, and within ten minutes two of the guns had been lost. However, the two remaining 18-pounders and their 'infantry' fought on until late afternoon against overwhelming odds. The survivors then retired in relatively good order after effectively delaying the German advance for 24 hours.

This encounter lends itself to gaming in 20mm scale. On the day, the 18-pounders were shooting at German armour over open sights, often firing point-blank at 100 yards range. There was plenty of infantry action too, with the British defending makeshift strongpoints, which were chiefly Bren and Lewis machine-gun positions in the upper windows of houses. In the game the defenders consisted of two 18-pounder field guns with ten crew plus 38 infantry figures armed with rifles, three Bren guns, and three Boys anti-tank rifles. I assume that the other two guns and a proportion of the infantry have already been lost and the only reinforcements that can be expected are a further fourteen infantrymen with two Bren guns. To win, the defenders must hold up the German advance for ten game moves. The British reinforcements are diced for on move five. A six-sided dice is thrown and a 5 or 6 indicates their arrival; If they do not materialize, then a further attempt is made with the dice on move six; and so on. It would be "unfair" to the British if all the attackers were to arrive on move one. This German arrival is regulated therefore into 'waves' of attackers. A chance factor is attributed to the appearance of each successive wave as indicated. German forces in the game comprise the following.

1st Wave, which starts from the edge of the table on German move one: three Panzer Is and a lorried infantry platoon (36 men).

2nd Wave: Two infantry sections (20 men) in two Sd Kfz 251/1 halftracks (Hanomags), a 75mm infantry howitzer and tow, plus two medium machine-guns in a light truck. These are diced for with a six-sided dice at the beginning of German move two. If 4, 5 or 6 are thrown they appear at the table edge; if 1, 2 or 3 are thrown they do not arrive but may be diced for on move three; and so on.

3rd Wave: Three Panzer 38(t)s, an infantry section (10 men) in a light truck, platoon HQ (6 men) in an Sd Kfz 251/10 halftrack (37mm anti-tank gun) and two 81mm mortars in a light truck. These are diced for on the move following the arrival of the second wave and with a similar chance of materializing.

4th Wave: two 150mm infantry howitzers plus tows, a vehicle repair/workshop unit and a senior command figure in a staff car. These are diced for on the move following the arrival of the third wave and with a similar chance of arriving.

The Germans' objective is to overrun the defenders or force them to withdraw from the village within the ten moves. My game was played on an 8ft × 5ft battlefield using various plastic buildings. Most commercial infantry/armour rules could be used to fight the action, but I suggest that morale factors be weighted in favour of the defenders in order to recreate the special 'flavour' of the engagement.

One facet of wargaming that appeals to many in the hobby is what might be called the 'What if'. Hindsight is a wonderful thing for the wargaming general. For example, the best documented Allied counter-attack took place at Arras. However, at the crucial moment Rommel appeared and rallied his troops, personally directing the anti-tank guns against the thickly armoured Matildas. What would have happened had he not been there? The French Air Force was notably misused, owing largely (as were most of the military failures) to the incompetence of the French High Command. The RAF actually lost more aircraft in combat than the French Air Force, although the former contributed only a fraction of the total strength. The swarms of Stukas, upon which blitzkrieg tactics relied heavily, would not have had it all their own way had the French used all the fighters they had to hand.

The defeat of the Allied armies in France has often been termed a flawed victory. Hitler himself had specifically ordered the annihilation of the BEF. What would have happened had the controversial 'halt' order not been given to Guderian's panzers? If the Germans had attacked the beleaguered British and French at Dunkirk, would the Allies have been able to influence what was to follow in central and southern France?

This brief view of wargaming the battles of May 1940 has been written with a personal bias towards recreating warfare with models. There are, however, several board games available, including Avalon Hill's *France 1940*, which provide off-the-shelf packages to play the campaign at strategic and tactical levels using maps and counters.

INDEX

Numbers in **bold** refer to illustrations

Aa Canal 85
aircraft production 19
Allied forces 13, 14, 16(table), 80
Altmayer, General 85
Amiens 80, 86
Ardennes, the 29, 30, 32, 38, 39
Arras 81, 82-83
Astier de la Vigerie, General Francois Pierre Raoul d'
    (1886-1956) 38, 39, 41, 49, 69, 80
Avesnes 70, 72

Bar, River 64
Barratt, Air Marshal 36, **37**, 69
Baudet, General 44, 57, 63
BEF <u>see</u> British Expeditionary Force
Belgian forces 13, 36, 38, 39, 45, 80, 86
Belgium 28, 29, 32-34
Beneditti, Major 58
Billotte, General Gaston Henri Gustave (1875-1940)
    9, 38, 41, 61, 64, 81, 83, 85
Blanchard, General Jean Georges Maurice
    (1877-1954) 38, 81
Bock, General Fedor von (1880-1945) 9, 30, 39
Brauchitsch, General Heinrich Alfred Walther von
    (1881-1948) 9, **10**
British Expeditionary Force 9, 13, 29, 38, 65, 77, 80, 81
    artillery **32-33**
    countattacks 82
    defence of Channel ports 85
    Dunkirk 85, 87, **89**
    withdraws to Haute Deule Canal 85
Brocard, General 67, 69
Bulson 57

Cambrai 77, **78-79**(map)
casualties 88
chronology 92-93
Churchill, Winston Leonard Spencer,
    First Lord of the Admiralty (1874-1965) **28**, 69,
    75-76
Corap, General Andre Georges (1878-1953) 35,
    61-62, 64, 69

de Gaulle, Colonel Charles Andre Joseph Marie
    (1890-1970) 73-74, 80, 86
dispositions 29, 30
Donchery 55-56
Dowding, Air Chief Marshall Hugh Caswell
    Tremenheere (1882-1970) 69

Dunkirk 85-87
Dutch army 13, 38, 39

Eben Emael 32-33
Flavigny, General 64, 67
France 6, 19, 27
Franklyn, Major-General 81, 82
French air force 6, 39, 41, 52, 65, 69, 76-77
    aircraft 15, **16**, 17, **36**
French army 6, 9, 19, 35-36, 37-38, 72, 86
    First Army Group 9, 16(table)
        First (Blanchard's) Army 29, 39, 85
        Second (Huntziger's) Army 17(table), 29, 44
        Sixth (Touch's) Army 69
        Seventh (Giraud's) Army 29, 38, 39, 77
        Ninth (Corap's)Army 17(table), 29, 67, 77
        1 Armoured Division 61, 66
        2 Armoured Division 69, 70, 77
        3 Armoured Division 64
        4 Armoured Division 73-74, 80
        artillery 15, **26**, **35**, **39**, 44, **49**, **58**, **60-61**, **65**
        defence of Meuse 45, 48, 49, 56-58
        losses 66, 69
        at River Bar 64
        at Sedan 44, 62-63
        situation, 16/17 May 75-76
        tanks 13, 15, **56-57**, 94
            Hotchkiss **12**, **48**, **73**
            Renault **2-3**, **13**, **14**, **40-41**, **84**
            'Somua' **12**

Gamelin, General Maurice (1872-1958) 8, 9, 34-35,
    36, 38, 48, 60, 80
        strategy 28-29
Georges, General Alphonse Joseph (1875-1951) 9, **9**,
    39, 41, 44, 60, 62-63, 64
        counterattacks 73, 74
        removes Corap from command 69
        on Sedan 48
German army 13, 31, 36-37, 39, 41, 67, 80
    Army Group 'A' 21(table), 30
        1 Panzer Division 37-38, 43-44, 54-55, 64, 69, 77
        2 Panzer Division 55-56, 56-57, 64, 69, 77, 80, 81
        5 Panzer Division 37, 66, 85
        6 Panzer Division 43, 75, 77
        7 (Rommel's) Panzer Division 43, 60-61, 62,
        65-66, 82
        8 Panzer 75
        10 Panzer Division 53, 77

Grossdeutschland Regiment 49, 54-55, 67, 69
Army Group 'B' 30
Army Group 'C' 30
armoured cars **55**, **62**
artillery **20**, **21**, **26**, 53, 69
halts on Aa Canal 85
infantry **37**, **53**, **63**, **75**, 76
losses 67
at the Meuse 44-45, **45**, 48-49, 53-56, 58-59
organisation 20(table), 24-25(table)
in Paris **90-91**
'special operations' 30
strategy 29-30
tactics 94-95
tanks 13, 15, 94
Pz Kpfw I Ausf B **30**
Pz Kpfw II **14**, **15**, **27**
Pz Kpfw III **71**, **91**
Sd Kfz 251/1 Ausf A **71**
Germany 27
Giraud, General Henri Honore (1879-1949) **8**, 69, 77
Gort, General Lord, 6th Viscount (1886-1946) **7**, **8**, **9**, **28**, 80, 81, 83, 85
Grandsard, General 44, 57, 58, 63, 86
Guderian, General Heinz Wilhelm (1888-1954) 10-11, **11**, 36, 43-44, 67, 80-81, 85
crosses Meuse 48-49
at Sedan 62, 63-64, 69-70
and von Kleist 44, 72-73

Haut-le-Wastia 48
Hitler, Adolf (1889-1945) 6-7, **7**, **10**, **29**, 30, 73, **90**
errors 88, 91
orders halt on Aa Canal 85
Holland 31-32, 38, 39, 59, 65
Hondeghem 95
Houx 43, 61
Huntziger, General Leon Clement (1880-1941) 35, 38, 41, 44, 57, 64

Ironside, General William Edmund (1880-1959) **9**, 81

Keitel, General Ewald von 9-10, **10**, **29**
Kleist, General Erwin von (1885-1954) **11**, **30**, 44, 72-73
Kluge, General Guenther Hans von (1882-1944) 70

Lafontaine, General 49, 57, 63
Leopold III, King of the Belgians (1901-83) 28, 83
List, General Siegmund Wilhelm (1880-1971) 72-73
Luftwaffe 31, 38, 41, 49, 76, 85, 87
aircraft 17-18
Junkers Ju 52 **31**
Junkers Ju 87 'Stuka' **18**, **52**, 52-53, **68**
Messerschmitt BF 109E-1 **18**, **22-23**, **41**
Luxemburg 31

Maastricht 38

Maginot Line, the **4-5**, 6, 13, 29, 70-72, **88**
Manstein, General Erich von (1887-1973) 30
Marfee Heights 49, 55, 57
Martin, General 43, 48, 62
Merdorp 59
Meuse, the 44-58, **46-47**(map), **50-51**(map), **52**
Molinie, General 85
Montcornet 70, 73
Montherme 59, 62, 67
morale 18-19, 27

Nouzonville 62

Onhaye 60-61

Paris 73, **90-91**
Poncelet, Colonel 57
prisoners of war 67, 72, 74, **81**, **89**
propaganda 19, 34

Raucourt 63
refugees **2-3**, 69, **70**, **76**, 77, 80, **84**
Reinberger, Major Hellmuth 28-29
Reynaud, Paul, French Prime Minister (1878-1966) 8, 69, 75-76
Rommel, General Erwin (1891-1944) 11, 36, 37, 43, 65-66, 70-72, 74, 85
advances to Cerfontaine 66-67
crosses the Meuse 44-45
delayed at Arras 81, 82-83
at Onhaye 60-61
takes Cambrai 77
Royal Air Force 36, 41, 49, 52, 65, 69, 87
aircraft 15, **16**, **17**, **36**, **60**, **86**
bombs Maastricht 38, 39
losses 31, 36, 38, 39, 41, 49, 65
Royal Navy 86-87
Rubarth, Feldwebel 53-54
Rundstedt, Field Marshal Karl Rudolf Gerd von (1875-1953) **9**, **10**, 30, 72-73

Sedan 44, 48-49, 52, 62-64, **66**(map), 67
Semois, the 38, 43
Sivry 70
Stonne 67, 69

theatre of operations **34**(map), **42**(map), **74**(map), **83**(map), **87**(map)
Touchon, General 69, 73, 77

uniforms **19**, **33**, **38**, **54**, **59**

wargaming 94-96
Wenzel, Sergeant-Major 33
Werner, Colonel 43
Weygand, General Maxime (1867-1965) 76, 80, 83
'Weygand Plan' 85
Wispelaere, Lieutenant de 43
Witzig, Lieutenant 33, 34